Breaking Free of PTSD

A copy of this publication can be found in the National Library of Australia.

ISBN 978-0-6482936-6-8 (paperback)

ISBN 978-0-6482936-7-5 (e-book)

Publisher: Cathie (Catherine) Anne Davies
Beyond PTSD

FORWARD

Both Neal and Cathie believe this book was something that needed to be written as a follow up to PTSD Not Just For Some But For Everyone. They have seen firsthand how the initial book has helped so many people through their journey either as a PTSD suffer or a Carer.

It was through their transparency and honesty of their lived experience that readers found a connection which broke down the barriers of self-judgement and loss of identify into their own living and/or lived experience by confirming to them that they're no longer alone on their journey.

ACKNOWLEDGEMENTS

Cathie and Neal would like to acknowledge and thank their amazing friends Phil and Valerie McGibboney for the support and encouragement they've given them, in the ongoing work their doing to help others through their challenging journey.

They'd also like to thank Valerie and Amy McGibboney for volunteering their time and effort to help with the proof reading of this book, along with a very special thank you to Helen Hendropurnomo, who also volunteered her time and effort, to oversee the final proof and editing of Breaking Free of PTSD.

Contents

Contents continued…

INTRODUCTION

BREAKING FREE OF PTSD is a follow-up to the 2019 book *PTSD Not Just For Some But For Everyone* by Neal Samuel Davies. The title *Breaking Free of PTSD* relates to a real-life story of how two married counsellors, Neal and Cathie, worked together over thirteen years to overcome Neal's chronic Post Traumatic Stress Disorder (PTSD).

In this book, we're not only going to focus on the techniques and strategies Neal used on his journey to free himself from his disorder, but also on the techniques and strategies Cathie used after she gave up her counselling career to become Neal's carer.

The actual premise of *Breaking Free of PTSD* is not to offer a cure, but to help both the person with PTSD and the carer, and to show them both that there can be a light at the end of the tunnel.

It's important to consider that this is an account of two career counsellors. The techniques and strategies they share are a result of years of prior studies and lived experience.

Both Neal and Cathie have written not only about what they did to help them get through their arduous journey, but they also emphasise that although many PTSD cases share similar symptoms, no two cases are the same. Each individual has unique characteristics, significant trauma and their own unique experience, which means some, will be affected more severely than others. They also point out that the overall effect of each trauma may vary for each individual, even when the traumas are almost identical. PTSD doesn't play favourites; it can affect any person, any time, after a traumatic incident. In this book, Neal and Cathie have shared pieces of their story and the tools and techniques that helped them. They've done this in the hope that someone experiencing trauma, or caring for those with trauma, will find a connection and see they're not alone on their journey. They also hope readers will find their own variations of the techniques and strategies Neal and Cathie used as they travelled through their own ordeal.

There are words and meanings that may recur as reminders throughout this book, because both Neal and Cathie felt it was imperative to get certain vital information across to you, the reader, especially for those who haven't read the previous book, which covers the first six years of Neal's chronic PTSD. Neal was working as a 'Relationship and Critical Incident Counsellor'. In his last six months of counselling, he attended approximately eleven critical incidents (helping save a man's life during one of them) but was later struck down with chronic PTSD. Cathie, his wife, was also a counsellor and she recognised just how bad her husband's disorder had been at the time, so she later gave up her career to become his carer.

In that previous book, Neal explained the emotional journey they'd both endured for six years and many of the techniques they'd used to get through the worst part of it, while still keeping their marriage intact. After a further seven years, it remains that way today. The only difference is that Neal is now counselling again.

THE ARDUOUS JOURNEY

Looking back to when Neal came crashing down with chronic PTSD, Cathie and Neal agreed that it was one of the most difficult situations they'd ever had to face in their entire relationship. They said that the lessons learned over that period bonded their love even more than in the entire thirty-three years they'd been together. Like the old saying goes, 'What doesn't kill you, makes you stronger!' There's no doubt that the journey they endured over a marathon thirteen years had not only made them stronger but further bonded their devotion to each other.

Many of the lessons they learned from lived experience built on the knowledge they'd gained from their studies and work as counsellors: simple things such as 'Don't blame yourself, or your partner, for this unforeseen event. It detracts from what you need to do to get through it. Self-blame won't improve the situation.'

Don't over-think situations or guess what the future may be - remain focused on one day at a time. Don't take things personally. That doesn't mean accepting negative put-downs, but try to keep situations calm, or walk away when emotions begin to override logical thought. Many lessons like this will be discussed in detail throughout the book.

In the early stages of his chronic PTSD, Neal's inability to cope with everyday life became overwhelming and made him emotionally unstable. He felt mentally weak and helpless. Neal was unable to control his everyday thoughts, and continually felt shame, guilt, and the loss of his identity. He described these overriding emotions as similar to large waves pounding constantly on a beach, with the sand lying there with no choice but to just take it. Neal was confused that he couldn't focus on the simplest of things or control his emotions, which made him feel that his entire life was out of control. He found it extremely difficult to hold back constant feelings of worthlessness. What was once his exceptionally clear-thinking process had now become blanketed with a haze of confusion, depression, anxiety and fear. The fear Neal faced was like nothing he'd ever faced before, causing him to isolate at home and later leave only with Cathie to attend appointments with his doctor, psychiatrist and psychologist.

After working with and helping so many clients with PTSD, Neal found it hard to believe that he could develop an extreme case of this debilitating disorder. As he puts it in his first book, on page 12, "PTSD doesn't discriminate; it doesn't matter if you're a rocket scientist, a builder, or a doctor, you're not immune to its sting or its control over your thinking and emotions."

The more Neal found himself incapable of controlling his emotions, the more he began to withdraw. His sleep patterns became constantly unstable, to the point that he was exceptionally lucky if he got four hours of sleep a night. This limited sleep was often broken by horrendous nightmares, which he explained were so vivid that it was difficult for him to tell whether he was still awake or asleep. This, of course, exacerbated his already heightened emotions and mental health. It was also detrimental to his physical health, to the point that he came down with a serious flu, something he hadn't had for years. In fact, he couldn't remember the last time he'd had one. The harder he tried to fight his chronic PTSD alone, the worse it became, and his self-esteem hit an all-time low.

Note: Whether you're a carer or a sufferer, you can't 'force' a person with PTSD to get better; it has to run its course.

When Neal's mind began venturing into uncharted waters, especially after eleven traumatic events, it became overloaded with confusion, leading to frustration. On top of that, he had flashbacks, serious anxiety and horrific nightmares, which had all been triggered by what he'd seen and heard first-hand.

PTSD, like any other invisible mental health disorder, is very hard for outsiders to understand or fully comprehend. People who don't have it and can't see it, often take the person with PTSD's anger and frustration as a personal attack on them. This admittedly isn't difficult to do if you haven't researched the symptoms of the disorder, so when Neal wrote his first book, he tried to give the reader examples of what he was feeling, to help those on the outside looking in, and here's one of those examples:

Imagine you’re wearing something soft on your feet, like socks, and then you drop a brick on your toe. No one’s going to see your pain or hear it - unless you’re screaming, of course. Why? Because your wound has no proof of existence; it becomes something only you can feel. The wound is there and you have to live with it, for as long as the pain persists. Now imagine feeling that emotional pain for most days of your life and then trying to act normally, masking your emotional pain,so you don’t feel that others will see you as odd, frustrated or angry with them.

This is what Neal was going through in what he called the 'Haze' and it lasted for just under two years from the beginning of his chronic PTSD.

The other way Neal described what he was going through was to ask others to imagine themselves trying to work out an almost unsolvable mathematical equation in their heads, while sitting in the middle of a ring of people, continually taking turns to yell out jumbled numbers that coincide with the problem they were trying to solve. At best, they have a matter of minutes to solve the problem. Then, to add to the dilemma, there is the sound of a very loud clock ticking, which is broadcast through a single earphone, given to them prior to the event. The single earpiece is to ensure the voices are loud and clear through the other ear. Not a very nice thought, is it? I believe most people would want to return to their usual normality as quickly as possible, but what happens when we're under this sort of enormous stress and frustration and can't return to our old normality? Well, Neal said, the moment he began to push his absolute desire to get back to normality to the extreme, all he did was make the chain reaction worse; by upping the overload, he said he'd upped his confusion, which then led him to more frustration and more anxiety. The only thing he said he'd achieved was further lack of focus.

HINTS ON WHERE TO START

Firstly, simplify your life by only doing the things you can do on a regular basis, whether it's getting your own breakfast every morning, feeding the dog every morning, writing notes about your feelings every day, researching PTSD every day or walking around your backyard every day. There's always something you can do on a regular daily basis that'll help make a positive difference to the goals you've set. If things are going well and you feel you can take on a larger goal, go for it, but if you try and it doesn't work out the first time, don't be disappointed. Be proud of yourself for giving it a go and then drop back down to where you were, or do something in between, or something less challenging than the one you just attempted, until you're ready to give the bigger one another try. Never be ashamed of giving something a go, just keep in mind the old fable of the Tortoise and the Hare: 'slow and steady wins the race'.

Let consistency be your focus. It can be very slow at times and it will try your patience, but you'll find impatience will let you down more times than being patient will, and if you persist with it, it will carry you all the way through. This habitual repetition is a great start and you can add more to it over time to keep yourself moving forward without stagnating.

Back in 2012, Neal was facing something he'd never faced before and didn't have the embedded emotional tools to fix the problem himself. The only way he'd managed to work through difficult issues in the past was to talk to those who were experienced in the mental health field and had a reasonable understanding of his disorder. Cathie mentioned there were times when it was exceptionally difficult to remove her focus from his anger or frustration and not respond negatively when she took his words as a personal attack. Although it was not an easy task, she'd shift her focus to listen effectively to what he was saying, not how he was saying it. The other thing she focused on was keeping herself calm while not being judgemental of his negative criticisms. All these things combined to help Cathie get Neal to trust her enough to move forward and eventually see a doctor. Cathie would also use reaffirmations with Neal from time to time, which helped reassure him he wasn't alone - simple sentences like: "I love you", "I'm not going anywhere", "I'm here for you", and most importantly, "We're in this together!" She also had a reasonable grasp of what he was going through and knew he needed more treatment than she could give him, including the possibility of some medication. Neal was initially hesitant, but he trusted her more than anyone else due to her approach. After a while, he cautiously allowed her to take him to see a doctor.

On his arrival at the doctor's office, the doctor gave Neal a test to check his mental state (which was terrible), and from there, he was sent to an amazing psychiatrist and later a psychologist. This was where Neal got help from the psychiatrist with both

medication and brainstorming through the issues he was facing. Neal also learned some new techniques that could help him at home.
The reason he trusted Cathie was not only because she was his wife, but also because of the way she used her knowledge and skills from being a counsellor by not pressuring him to communicate.

Note: Learn what makes them feel safe without pushing them into something they're not ready for, by observing their reactions.

Something Cathie wants to make very clear is that it's one thing to go to work and do counselling, but another to look after your loved one and not be affected one way or another.
During the 'Haze' period, Cathie explained that the symptoms she was observing and facing from her own perspective were very personal. Cathie's first observation was how very sad Neal seemed, and she likened it to someone mourning the loss of a

loved one. He constantly looked sad and communication was almost gone, which deeply concerned her. Doubts crept into her head that perhaps he might do something drastic, even though she knew his deep Christian faith wouldn't allow him to do that, yet she couldn't help worrying about his state of mind.

Initially Cathie saw Neal's withdrawal from her as simple tiredness. They'd both been like ships in the night and their jobs had expectations of them travelling hundreds of kilometres a week and sleeping over while counselling a couple of nights a week. So it was quite the norm by the time the weekend came for him to be exhausted, but once his chronic PTSD set in, she began to see additional major changes in Neal. Neal wasn't coping at all and frustration was building within him, which brought about 'sharp and to the point' answers whenever she'd ask him questions. This was definitely out of character for Neal, and he finally broke down, saying he couldn't go on doing what he had been doing!

Cathie deliberately repeats this, so other carers understand.

"What was extremely important at this point was that I understood that his mood swings weren't a deliberate attack on me, nor was his irritability; it was all part of his symptoms, symptoms I'd seen many times in others I'd worked with who had PTSD, so rather than taking his emotional attitude and words personally, I had to shut down my routine focus on what was a very happy marriage and refocus on what would be the best way to help Neal, whose personality seemed to have changed overnight."

During the early stages of Neal's journey, Cathie felt that forcing him to talk to her about the details of what happened would be a mistake, as she didn't feel it was appropriate at that time and could possibly make him feel worse than he already felt. So instead, she explained to him it wasn't necessary for him to talk to her about what he'd seen and/or heard on those eleven separate occasions, but she did ask him to tell her what he was feeling in the here-and-now, so she could understand his present feelings.

Both Neal and Cathie were facing personal issues they'd never encountered individually or as a couple before, and it frustrated both of them to no end. They found that neither of their needs or concerns on certain matters were being met. For example, when Neal was having enormous difficulty thinking clearly and had trouble explaining what he was feeling, it didn't seem to matter what Cathie did to try and help him; it would only cause further frustration for him. Deep down inside, Neal knew Cathie was doing all she could to help fix the problem, but the turmoil of pent-up frustration going on within him would eventually overwhelm him and boil over into comments like, "You have no idea what I'm going through!", "I really don't want to talk!" or "Please, just let me be!"

Cathie was finding it extremely frustrating as well and realised the most positive way she could deal with it was to back off and only respond when Neal had a question or made a statement, and even then, she'd keep her replies to a minimum. She also found it extremely difficult to accept this new persona Neal had unwillingly adopted; it was hard for her to believe a man who had such amazing communication skills and was so involved and loving of life, could shift so quickly into becoming self-isolating and barely communicative. The initial adjustments Neal and Cathie had to make needed to be done in an extremely short time, which made it even more overwhelming for both of them.

It was so important that Cathie didn't get bogged down and allow the presenting issues to enter her thoughts and create negative predictions for her future, so she made a solid decision to focus on making a shift to positive solutions. So when Neal felt he wasn't handling things too well after his recent trauma, Cathie convinced him to see his doctor and she accompanied him, so he'd feel safe. Cathie also expressed to him that he shouldn't feel he was any less of a person after he was later referred to a psychiatrist.

REVIEW: NEAL'S EARLY STAGES OF HIS CHRONIC PTSD

In most instances, PTSD doesn't normally establish itself over a long period of time such as years. It will usually come on in days, weeks or months. This makes it very difficult for someone caught up in a traumatic incident to have the time to get on top of it immediately. Mind you, some people aren't affected at all and others are affected to the furthest extreme. Imagine saying to someone who's just lost a limb in an accident to "get over it", a week or two after it happened, or even a month after it happened? Just because you can't see the PTSD issues doesn't mean they're not there or any less traumatic than the person who's lost the limb. We all need time to adjust to something that's very new to us and at times it makes us very anxious, but eventually you learn how to work through what you need to do and the anxiety dies down.

Imagine not being able to think through practically anything. Imagine someone smashing your fingers with a rock or hammer but there's no pain, yet the emotions coming from that incident are almost identical or even worse. On top of that, you're caught within yourself with constant anxiety and no answers or way of resolving the problem. Can you imagine that?

Consider this: *most* psychologists and counsellors working in the field of trauma or critical incidents, and/or others such as firemen, paramedics etc., who've worked within traumatic situations, require what's called debriefing. This means these experienced workers, who've heard horrific stories of the traumatic event or have been first responders and witnessed the aftermath of those events, require another specialist to listen as they verbally release the impact of their experiences, so they don't become PTSD victims themselves. The issue here is that many of the family members or friends may also be told of these horrific and traumatic events from those who are suffering and want or need to unload on someone close to them.

The person listening may emotionally feel some of their loved one's PTSD pain and then feel a sense of hopelessness and helplessness about helping or comforting them, because they don't have the training in this field. On top of this, most family members are reluctant to seek help because of how they may be seen by others and then feel guilty because it wasn't they themselves who went through the trauma/s, and the person who did needs the help and attention, not them.

THE EFFECTS OF LOSING COMMUNICATION

If PTSD occurs after a traumatic event, the ability to communicate with others can diminish enormously. When Neal was in what he called the 'Haze', which came with his chronic PTSD, after attending numerous critical incidents as an on-site counsellor where he was often confronted with trauma at close quarters, PTSD began to reduce his ability to communicate until it almost disappeared entirely. Neal was frustrated to the point of becoming irritable and seriously withdrawn. The question of how someone can then communicate with others while going through these issues became an extremely difficult one.

Neal said, “I don’t think I’ve ever had so much difficulty communicating with others, including my wife and family, as I did during the worst of my PTSD, and even when I felt I could, the conversations were kept to a bare minimum!” Neal went on to explain that the majority of his conversations were possible during moments when he felt calmer than normal and his breathing was at a slow and steady pace. Mostly, these rare moments came after he'd been writing, painting, or jotting down in his journal how he was travelling emotionally each day. All these small distractions had a calming effect that eventually enabled him to communicate more and more as time went on.

Cathie stated that when Neal wanted to communicate, she'd make sure they'd retreat to what they call their 'Coffee Nook.' The Coffee Nook is a small cosy, quiet room that adjoins their kitchen, where they make cappuccinos and sit and read or have conversations in the mornings before doing anything else. Cathie always felt it was the best place for him to 'open up' because there were fewer distractions such as TV, computers or outside noises, and he'd always commented prior to PTSD, how relaxed he'd felt there.

Cathie focused on allowing Neal to do most of the talking and very rarely made long, drawn-out statements, so when she spoke it was mostly brief and to the point. She'd listen long and hard to what Neal had to say and also watch his facial expressions, so she'd know when to pull back if she felt she was asking too many questions of him. Once Neal felt slightly uncomfortable or agitated, he'd say to Cathie, "I really need to stop now." They would agree to continue the conversation at a later time.

None of this type of communication was comfortable for either of them, but when you love and care for someone and are both trying to push through a very difficult time, you don't want to surrender what has temporarily gone, but improve on what you have.

After Neal came out of his 'Haze', he commented that when he was speaking to Cathie, he often felt as though he'd over-talked to the point of prattling on and was tremendously embarrassed by this; he felt, as a counsellor, he'd been self-programmed to listen to others and not over-speak to the point that the other person rarely got a word in. It was then that he began to understand just how good a counsellor his wife was and how much work she'd put in to help him communicate his feelings to her, which in turn had helped him move forward and out of the 'Haze'.

When Neal was in the depths of his PTSD, he definitely didn't want to be pushed into anything, as his own inner frustration of not being able to help himself confused and frustrated him even more. So, if someone he depended on, like Cathie, had tried to force him into something he'd already desperately tried to do himself, but wasn't yet capable of doing, the healing process would probably have taken even longer, and his condition might have worsened. By Cathie being patient and allowing Neal to feel he had some sort of control, where he felt he had none, he began to move forward. Cathie makes the very important point that directives wouldn't have helped Neal at all. However, listening and engaging as a team-member reduced Neal's sense of being alone on his journey and helped him to feel more comfortable about sharing his feelings. In other words, if a person directs someone who's lost the ability to comprehend clearly, then the frustration of wanting to but not being able to do so heightens their discomfort and sets them back, but effectively listening and having fewer expectations makes their journey a little easier. Also, they're more likely to open up about their feelings to someone they sense is on the journey with them.

Ask yourself this: "Do I like being pushed into something at a time when I've got a lot of other things going on in my head?"

We often assume what others want without actually listening to or asking them what they want. For example, someone has bacon and eggs every morning for breakfast, but on this occasion they inform us the night before that they have a tummy bug, yet the following morning, we've cooked their breakfast as usual, thinking they'd be over the bug by now, but they're not, and now we're disappointed, plus a little angry that they won't eat it. We're even further frustrated when we find out no one else wants it and both our time and the food have been wasted. The only way to know what someone is truly thinking is through communication, and communication isn't just talking but effective listening as well.

Recapping the Dos and Don'ts

Both: Don't focus on a time limit for recovery.

Some people suffering from PTSD may recover more quickly than others. Cathie found with Neal that the more she pushed for a quick recovery, the more frustration and setbacks it caused him, so she learned very quickly to back off, and it was then, and only then, that he began to move forward.

Carers: Don't take things said by them as a personal attack on you.

People with PTSD may not always have control over their emotional behaviour and will sometimes respond negatively when trying to communicate through their own internal frustration and anxiety.
Carers: Allow them to communicate on their terms.

Cathie knew from her experience as a counsellor that whenever you push a client too hard, they'd often pull back, and communication would fall away.
When a child throws a tantrum, you can't always get through to them via communication, as their emotions override their logical thinking. So, often parents wait until they're calm. The same may apply to someone who's in pain (emotional and/or physical) and is sobbing uncontrollably. Sometimes speaking softly to them helps, but on many occasions they say they want to be left alone, and

you'll need to revisit the issue when they're ready to talk. What we must remember is that they need to talk on their terms. It's not only about what we want to know, but more importantly, what they want us to know, as they may feel uncomfortable speaking about hurtful things that have happened. If forced to relive it, they may lose trust in us for making them talk about something they're not ready to face.

Carers: Try to be supportive but not patronising.

Patronising someone with PTSD can actually make them feel foolish, especially if that person, prior to the incident, had a responsible, mature and independent personality. This particular person has gone from being able to solve issues competently, to someone who has trouble thinking through the simplest of problems due to their emotional state.

Patronising can set them back emotionally, as they're already struggling with not being able to cope in ways they once could. On top of everything else, they're also being bombarded with negative thoughts, which makes them feel less than the person they once were. So, sometimes patronising can convince them of their own negative thoughts.

Carers: Don't be pushy by making them do things they don't feel they can do.

What Cathie realised she was doing, and then immediately stopped, was being pushy, which had a similar outcome to being patronising when it comes to someone with PTSD.

Once you start pushing them to do things that they're not ready to do, they relapse into a negative state, and Neal once said to Cathie, "Don't you think I feel foolish enough that I can't do it?"

From that moment on, Cathie would ask Neal, "Do you feel like…?" or "Would you like to…?"

Some of these things may seem difficult for you, but compared with what many PTSD sufferers are going through, these are 'a walk in the park'.

TRAPPED AND WANTING TO BREAK FREE, YET FEARFUL TO DO SO

NEAL

Since Cathie and I began speaking to groups on the subject of PTSD, I've had so many people approach me, and I could immediately see in them the confusion and anxiety that I myself felt throughout my journey.

The thing is, most people with this disorder identify with others who also have it, even though each case is significantly different; each person has their own unique personality, and they perceive their trauma completely differently from others, even if those others experienced the same trauma.

So, symptoms of PTSD may vary extremely, in their effect, from one person with the disorder to another, while the daily persistence of the symptoms may also vary on a 'more or less' basis.

So even if three people are in the same car when an accident occurs, their responses to trauma may be totally different from each other; one person may have flashbacks and nightmares, another may suffer from extreme anxiety and/or anger, and the other may be shaken up, but not affected at all.

The one similarity I've found in those suffering from PTSD, that I've spoken to individually, is that 99% of them have overall feelings of being caged in their inner-self and want to break free from this cage as quickly as they possibly can. These sufferers have no idea how to break free, and the harder they try and fail, the more frustrated and withdrawn they become.

I once described this feeling as accidentally hitting your finger with a hammer, or accidentally spilling scalding water on yourself, and then someone comes to you and keeps asking over and over if you're ok?

All of a sudden you don't feel like saying 'I'm fine', but more like telling them to shut the heck up, and even though you don't have the extreme pain of the hammer hitting your finger, you do have that same extreme emotional sensation to be left alone.

CATHIE

What we often overlook in most cases of trauma is what family members or friends are going through as well, so I asked Cathie what she was feeling in the initial stages of Neal's chronic PTSD.

"Honestly, I was struggling with my own personal problems and would have enormous trouble discussing them. How can you even consider talking about your own emotional issues, when someone you love is going through hell? You certainly want to, but at the same time you feel like you're drowning in self-guilt, so you really couldn't discuss them with anyone!"

Cathie made it very clear that she definitely couldn't discuss her issues with Neal because of the additional burdens it would place on him. How can someone so close cope, or feel like going to work, while stressing over what might happen while they're there? Especially when you're financially strapped, and you know it would only create more problems for both of you if you didn't. She went on to say, "It's very easy to withdraw into yourself and just function."

Just functioning wasn't all that happened. Without her knowing, she began to lose her identity. She said she was so focused on Neal's chronic PTSD, that her life was engulfed in it. Protecting Neal meant everything to her, to the point of her nurturing him, while the focus on her career and other things she loved doing, all of a sudden, became a selfish ideal.

Cathie said her feelings and thoughts became a little erratic at times, angry that this had happened to Neal, angry that it had happened to her, hurt and sad for Neal, and missing the person she once loved, still loved, and patiently waiting for him to come back. She also felt alone and isolated, due to Neal not wanting to go anywhere or do anything.

Neal would tell Cathie to go out, but she felt guilty that he was stuck there, inside himself, alone in the house.

As Neal began to come out of his 'Haze', Cathie found herself floundering with the loss of her own identity. Neal had desperately needed her throughout the early stages of his PTSD, but once he'd begun clawing his way back, she felt like she was being pushed aside, which would bring about some very mixed emotions, such as slight resentment, loss of purpose, relief and at times a numbness.

Cathie understood that this was nowhere near full recovery, but it was still very different from what she was used to. Neal was self-isolating, and now he was pushing himself to overcome the constant issues he'd been facing for so long. He was still having horrific nightmares, anxiety attacks and flashbacks. Some of his focus had returned, but he was determined to regain it all.

Neal continued to focus on distractions when it came to many of his PTSD issues, so Cathie felt if it worked for him, why couldn't it work for her? So she began collecting and learning about toys she'd never had as a child, she began studying antiques and collectables. Cathie would take Neal with her to garage sales and flea markets, until at last she'd also broken down the barriers that were creating her loss of identity.

Cathie says (without any resentment) she'd gone through and hidden so much from Neal and others to the point that she'd become lost in the midst of Neal's PTSD, and somewhere along the way, she'd left a piece of herself behind. Every single thing she did, she did for Neal without questioning, 'What about me?'

Reflecting back, she now gives a word of advice to other loved ones of people with PTSD: "Do what I did, but before you do it, write yourself a note and hold on to it throughout your journey. The note should read, *'Remain aware of my feelings and identity, and make sure I find things to do for myself. If and when I start to feel an overload, and if it all becomes too much, I must get help from a professional and talk it out."*

There is so much Cathie has learned from this journey, and it doesn't matter how strong you are, or think you are. A journey like the one Neal and Cathie faced has to leave some scarring, but as Cathie sees it, 'What journey in life doesn't? Even more importantly, it also gives us the opportunity to learn valuable lessons that we can take in and then pass on to others.'

THE BREAKTHROUGH

As time went by and Neal began to improve, he still desperately longed to go back to his career of counselling and Cathie needed to slowly sway him temporarily away from that objective and toward another. The emphasis on slowly is due to the disorder; if she'd pushed him too hard and/or too quickly, it would have ended in a negative result and a backward step in his recovery.

Once a fortnight, they'd do their shopping and most times Neal would want to find a coffee shop where they could sit in an inconspicuous corner, but also where he could watch others and feel like he was actually participating in life again. To Neal, this was like a convict being released from an internal gaol cell, being still unsure of how to handle what was mentally being thrown at him, like panic attacks, hyper-sensitivity to noise, flashbacks and small memory lapses. Each time he'd go to the shopping centre, he'd set himself new challenges. Most of these challenges were focused on overcoming his anxiety attacks, which were due to flashbacks of past traumatic incidents. Neal taught himself how to use numerous distraction techniques, like focusing on his car keys and imagining he was driving to a place he loved, such as the beach, until his anxiety slowly settled down and he could recognise what feature was connected to previous trauma and then deal with it. These techniques worked so well that he got to the point where he'd rarely have flashbacks and his anxiety attacks began to lessen. Mind you, nothing happens overnight; it all takes time, practice and patience. We also need to remember that his condition was diagnosed as chronic and no one really expected him to come as far as he eventually did.

Later, when Neal began to focus on the issues surrounding his hyper-sensitivity to noise (Hyperacusis), he'd ask Cathie to sit with him and have lunch at the noisiest possible spot. At first, they'd sit there and leave immediately after they'd eaten, when Cathie would ask, "Are you ok? You've turned as white as a ghost." She could see Neal's anxiety was going through the roof, and she knew it was time to move on. Week after week, month after month, year after year, his hyper-sensitivity to noise has reduced, and it occurs only on the rarest of occasions. It can now be contained within, rather than overflowing into watery eyes and shaky hands. Neal never suggests that others should push themselves to these extremes and reiterates that he did this little by little, bit by bit, until he was ready for the next step and if he didn't feel ready for it, he wouldn't do it. What's important here is having enough awareness to know your limitations and to create a habitual weekly programme that you're comfortable with, until you're ready to push your boundaries one step further. Only you will know what you're ready for and if it's too overpowering. Don't be afraid to take a step back and work at something you're comfortable with. Once you have awareness, you should have the knowledge to make better decisions. If at any time you feel indecisive, talk it out with those who know you well enough, so they can help you put things into a clearer perspective. If you're seeing a psychologist at this time, he or she would be the ideal person to speak to.

Neal's main priority was to treat his PTSD as his competitor, not his master. Even when we compete, we still have to learn basic skills and rules in order to enter the competition, otherwise we would scramble around without focus and get nowhere. Because of Neal's condition, his strategies needed to be very basic. When it came to Neal's PTSD, learning the basic dos and don'ts was the key. Slow deep breaths worked with many of the symptoms he had in the initial stages, especially when anxiety hit him during horrific nightmares, flashbacks and even just leaving the house. There are myriad things we can all do, but more importantly, it's better not to overload yourself by thinking you can do them all at once or on your own all the time, and as hard as it is in the beginning, it really is important to learn to share the load by talking with others.

Many of the tools Neal writes about were used after he came out of his initial 'Haze'. His first awareness of getting any slight semblance of thinking clearly was after having a number of visits with a psychiatrist and later finding an excellent psychologist after two attempts. So, if you feel you’re suffering from dissociation or disconnection from others while going through PTSD, he encourages you to make an appointment with a doctor, who may in turn refer you to a specialist, who understands your disorder.

Once you’re through the 'Haze', a simple but helpful method Neal used was, and still is, repetition; Neal used this by getting up at the same time every morning, feeding the chickens, preparing the coffee machine and reading two or more pages of the Bible. Once Cathie was up, she’d feed the dogs and prepare their coffee. While having their morning coffee, they'd sit and talk. Later in the morning, Neal would get on the computer and write or research, while Cathie would do similar or she’d go outside in the garden. At lunchtime, they’d sit and watch a programme on TV together and then return to what they were previously doing. This may sound like a boring day to some, but for Neal and

Cathie, where there was once nothing to get up for, their motivation to actually do something together and be able to minimally communicate on a better level, gave their lives a new sense of hope and positive purpose.
Routine gave Neal back some self-worth and also gave him drive to accomplish more. If he'd allowed himself to consider that these menial, routine tasks he was doing were futile, then he believes he'd be creating his own victim mentality and blocking what was a positive way forward. Sometimes we have to crawl before we can walk and without doing that, we can never learn to stand on our own two feet.

Note: Sometimes putting our pride before our small achievements can block larger achievements that make us proud.

Neal had always told Cathie to look for patterns when working with clients and now that she'd become Neal's carer, she had to change her own thoughts on how she'd go about working through this new relationship. Neal's prior advice eventually helped her to see that each time she'd tried to push him forward, he'd take a step back and the pattern became obvious, which also became frustrating for both of them. Like anything else, living in a loving relationship can also consist of habitual rituals and emotional feelings and to change anything that's habitual can also become uncomfortable.

While considering what to do next, Cathie reflected on her younger days when she had her first child. Although this was enormously different from what was happening in her and Neal's lives now, there were some interesting similarities that she believed required further investigation. These similarities were: **she had more dependence** placed on her from someone she loved, **she had more frustration** and stress due to an additional workload, **she had more demands** made on her emotional well-being and the feeling of whether or not she could remain patient with the ongoing situation and **she had more thoughts** of 'Am I doing this right?' or 'Am I failing?'

Once Cathie had put in place these comparisons, she realised an integral part of helping Neal would be to remain patient, not overload herself with stress and not expect a fast recovery but have a 'one day at a time' attitude. When Cathie stopped pushing changes and stopped putting pressure on herself to do better, positive things began to happen for both of them. She'd only approach Neal with specific issues and would always reply quietly and calmly, while keeping her answers short and to the point. Even if Neal got aggravated over something, she'd approach the situation with less stress and in the above manner.

Imagine the frustration of someone trying to change a tyre while in a hurry to get somewhere and the nut on the wheel won't loosen. It's often not until that person walks away from the vehicle and calms themselves down, that they can even consider emotionally working through another way of loosening it off. Now imagine their loved one, seeing their frustration and feeling helpless to help them, knowing if they do, it could infuriate them further. In these scenarios, it helps us understand that the more frustrated we get over negative events, the more it can cause our emotions to shoot up and override our logical thinking. The best thing we can do for ourselves and others at this point is take a step back until we calm down and regain our composure and then think through what we need to do. Being in a hurry and expecting to fix an issue when frustration has crept in will only cloud our thought process further. This also applies to those who see the emotional pain their loved one is going through and want to help but don't realise the best way to help them, is sometimes to not help them until they call on it from you.

All through Neal's horrific ordeal, Cathie remained amazingly patient waiting for him to open up, and she continued to resist pushing him ahead too quickly. Part of her strategy was to avoid Neal, and although this may seem insensitive, over time it created a desire from Neal to communicate. Even with her focus on less communication, she would still keep some of their old normality in play by asking him what he'd like for lunch or dinner, but if there was anything else he required, she'd mostly leave that for him to approach her and then respond in a manner that would be calm and to the point. Cathie also spent much of her spare time working in the garden. When Neal was going through quiet spells, she'd pop into the house from time to time to check on him, or when she felt like a cup of coffee or tea herself, and while she was inside, she'd ask him if he wanted one too. If he said no, she'd leave it at that and not bother him with further conversation. Cathie mostly waited for Neal to communicate with her, so she could respect his boundaries rather than vice versa, and this seemed to work well, but in her own mind she still had concerns for the permanency of his disorder. It felt emotionally straining to hold back her feelings, and she'd often sit quietly on her own and reflect on what she could have done better to avoid what had happened to him, but in reality, there really wasn't anything she could have done any better, and to dwell on it could only make things worse for both of them, so she continued to push forward in the hope that there would eventually be change.

Her message to others is, "Try to stay calm and manage your responses whenever spoken to abruptly; also, create your own personal routine around the home, but always answer when they speak, and when you do, be short and to the point in a calm voice."

She found that by doing this, it would enhance the curiosity within Neal and would improve his eagerness to communicate with her. Simply put, Cathie had learned to invite Neal to participate, rather than push him into it; if it didn't interest him, she realised she needed to let it go, rather than push to make him respond to her own requests. The more she did this, the more Neal felt excluded and also felt the need to participate more. This, by no means, says she stopped caring for him; she didn't, and this may not work in every case of PTSD, but this is what Neal says helped him through the very worst of his chronic condition.

Note: Lifestyle changes can initially be uncomfortable, but over time they eventually become the norm.

Once Cathie and Neal had entered this new phase, Neal was still years from full recovery, and now Cathie had to adjust her approach. Even though Neal had recovered some of his clear-thinking capacity, there were still, at times, overriding anxieties and depression which continued to keep him reserved and withdrawn, and even though he was now leaving the house, there were also certain triggers that would cause anxiety and flashbacks. Neal was in a place where he felt a little more comfortable with having Cathie with him, and also a little more open to communication. During the times they did communicate, Cathie remained calm when getting to the point, and also continued to be direct. When asking Neal questions, Cathie kept the questions brief, rather than drawing them out. Cathie also felt it was time for Neal to communicate a little more, but she knew at the same time she couldn't overload him. Cathie explained to Neal that if he was feeling uncomfortable at any point in their conversation, he'd just have to simply tell her. Following that, they could both take a time-out, and come back to the conversation whenever he was ready. Cathie explained that this took the pressure off him trying to push through both words and emotions.

Neal keeps reminding others not to put a time limit on their PTSD. He says this was so important for him to know, but he didn't discover it in the early stages. Once he made that discovery, he began to move forward.

Neal made the decision that the best pathway to clear-thinking, as he came out of the first stage of PTSD, was to put his extreme desires for him to return to his career on pause and reconsider what he could do in the here-and-now, rather than what he could do before the disorder hit him. This new focus was entirely different from his initial instinct of pushing forward as hard and quickly as possible. Neal found that all this pushing did was hold him back and frustrate his unstable emotional mind further, and the more pressure he put on himself to return to work, the longer it took to come out of the initial stage, which he called the 'Haze'. This early period lasted almost two years and taught him some very hard lessons, which only became clear to him after the event.

Note: When we consider two different perspectives from two individuals craving the same outcome, we can then gather the issues which prevent advancement and collectively work as a team to overcome them.

Cathie pointed out that, like any other couple, they'd had their normal ups and downs, but being counsellors, they'd always continued to communicate their feelings and resolve their issues, but this time was different. This time Neal's entire persona had dramatically changed, and he'd become totally withdrawn from the world - irritable, moody, anxious, depressed and frightened all rolled into one, the total opposite of the person who had one day gone off to work and returned as another, and all she could think of was, she wanted her old Neal back! When she saw the pain in his eyes from this once emotionally strong man, she could see he was completely broken, and her heart fell to her feet. She felt confused and helpless, and once he received his diagnosis, she felt even more mixed emotions such as unacceptance, anger and yet also felt relieved of self-blame, knowing she hadn't contributed to what he had. At this early point, Cathie began to nurture him, and that proved a positive strategy, right up until he started coming out of the 'Haze', but once out, Neal became irritated by it and explained his feelings and how he'd regained a lot of focus, and he felt he needed to do some things for himself. Although this was hard for Cathie to accept after almost two years, she knew it was important for him and immediately stopped.

Another really important thing Neal and Cathie both learned from the 'Haze' and adapted and encompassed into their lives after it, was to go at their own pace, which was something they hadn't done initially, when both of them desperately wanted this horrendous nightmare to finish as quickly as possible. They soon found out that this strategy definitely doesn't work with PTSD. As mentioned before, many PTSD journeys won't last as long as theirs did, depending on the symptoms, of course. One thing Neal and Cathie did, which they believe will help others get through their initial stages, as carers and/or those with the disorder, was to accept that they couldn't fix it overnight. Find a steady pace rather than rushing to break down the barriers of PTSD too quickly.

Awareness was everything to both Neal and Cathie. In the initial part of the journey, Neal had very little awareness and was mostly living day to day on emotion and reaction, but as his awareness and thought process slowly came back, he could plan and resist the temptation of pushing himself beyond his capabilities, and also explore ways of dealing with the things that needed to be done. This awareness continued to keep him on track when his instincts kicked in, and when they tried to push him too quickly back to his old normality, he'd immediately pull back and stick to the plan.

Note: Impatience can create lost opportunities and setbacks, but awareness of limitations can keep a steady plan moving forward.

While talking to and working with many PTSD sufferers, since getting through his own chronic PTSD, they have said that, like Neal, in the early stages, they felt very alone and uncomfortable around other people. Neal, who doesn't directly compare himself with other PTSD sufferers, indicates to them how he felt when he was going through the initial stages of his own disorder. He explains to them that he felt like he was suffering from an Inferiority Complex on top of the many other symptoms he had. He makes it very clear that this isn't done as a comparison with what they're going through, nor is it a sympathy grab, but talking about it helps to create a bond. Let me explain: when Neal gently and thoughtfully points out the complexity of what he went through, it has an almost immediate effect, creating mixed emotions. On one hand, their facial expressions seem at first confused, but then they become one of knowing and immediate connection, which can present as a smile and/or tears of relief, leading to acceptance.

At this point, Neal withdraws from speaking and becomes the emotional sounding board for these other PTSD sufferers. They can then pour out their own stories that they couldn't express to others before him. Once they've let it all out, he reassures them that they're not alone. He also informs them that approximately 11% of Australians have PTSD, and even though they're all individual cases, each person Neal speaks with has many of the same symptoms as these other 11% of Australians.

REMAINING PATIENT AND CREATING PERSONAL TIME-OUT

Note: Giving control back where control has been lost can rebuild confidence.

Neal and Cathie also created an inconspicuous signal, where Neal would hold both his hands up, with palms out from his chest to let her know when to stop. This helped Neal to feel more in control, and led to more communication.

Note: If PTSD is the enemy, then it's always better to face the enemy with an army than to face it alone.

Cathie's journey was a very difficult one, yet at the end of it, it was also rewarding even though there were times when her stress levels were high. This often happened when she'd find herself apologising for speaking too loudly at a café or almost anywhere they went out in public, and she couldn't understand why. Neal was also confused, as he couldn't understand why Cathie was raising her voice in public. Whenever she spoke, the sound cut through his emotional senses like a razor-sharp knife. Neal could see his wife becoming stressed over this issue and felt he needed to do more research regarding his disorder. He found a condition called Hyperacusis, which can be caused by PTSD and can make normal sounds unbearably loud.

Once Neal had the answer, he felt more at ease when they were out and if Cathie's voice seemed louder than normal, he'd use breathing techniques to lower his anxiety. Once fully aware of what was really happening, he was astonished to find that when he lowered his anxiety with his breathing techniques, what initially seemed like an extremely high-pitched quality in Cathie's voice would lower in volume. There were other times, too, when Cathie would begin to feel stressed, unsettled or confused. This also created self-doubt, leading to losing a lot of her self-confidence. Neal might drop something on the floor and although he never blamed Cathie, he'd storm out of the room incredibly angry with himself, sometimes calling himself stupid and useless. Later he would come back in and apologise for his behaviour. This would also happen when he would have mental blanks while trying to explain something to Cathie. Much of the time, Cathie would feel like she was walking around on eggshells.

Neal was never abusive toward Cathie, just frustrated with himself and his own capability to do simple tasks. So, although he'd come out of the 'Haze', she could still see that some of the original symptoms remained. Cathie reminded herself not to take what he was doing or saying as a personal attack but to see it for what it was.

Neal and Cathie had been together over thirty years and Neal had never threatened or laid a hand on Cathie in anger or spite. She knew he'd give his life to save hers. Yes, they'd definitely had arguments over the years; there was never personal abuse of any sort. Their arguments were always about the subject they were debating.

FEELINGS OF INFERIORITY AND OTHER SYMPTOMS

As Neal reflects back on that time, he remembers having feelings of inadequacy and insecurity. He also had trouble remaining calm or capable of managing responses when a question was asked of him. There's no doubt he was feeling embarrassed by his condition and didn't want to go anywhere because he thought that people would think less of him because of the emotional issues he was having.

He continually asked himself how people would perceive a person who is supposed to help others through this disorder and yet can't help, or cope, by himself! Neal couldn't understand why he felt that way back then, but in hindsight he can clearly see what he needed to do. Whenever he's talking to clients, he continues to make these suggestions and asks these questions of them, "We all give others our advice when we see that they need it, so why do we find it so hard to accept advice from others who are thinking much clearer than we are and with more awareness of our situation? Isn't that why we have teachers, coaches and instructors, etc.? There are people who aren't as smart as we are, but that doesn't mean they can't give us suggestions or have some minimal amount of comprehension of what we're going through. If we're that desperate to get back on track, isn't it possible that some of the things they tell us may lead to further expansion of our own thoughts on these matters?"

Surprisingly, Neal found that loose-fitting, comfortable clothes helped comfort him when it came to dealing with his Inferiority Complex. The clothing made him feel a little more relaxed and at times cosy, as a warm fire does on a cold night. Any little thing he thought might help, including what he'd learned when studying to become a counsellor, as well as considering the things that had comforted him on his journey through life, would all intertwine to create a new way through what he was facing. He believed if he could get his brain habitually focusing on the things that had calmed him throughout his life, he could also use them as a distraction whenever things were at their worst.

Note: Helping someone to place focus on what they can do, rather than what they can't, can redirect their negatives to positives.

When someone is having flashbacks or nightmares and feels like others are seeing him or her as less than, it becomes exceptionally difficult to be forthcoming, not only when communicating, but the extreme characteristics of these symptoms can also lead to the fear of leaving the home.

The further he went along, Neal learned to take one deep breath through his nose and exhale it out of his mouth. This helped to not only calm himself down, but also to move thoughts and focus from frustrated feelings to his breathing, which then became a positive distraction and a road to better communication.

So, as you can see, whenever Neal had time alone and felt ready to push forward, he didn't want to be idle and therefore looked for any information he could find on the internet regarding PTSD. Finding this information didn't mean he was going to discard his psychiatrist's input at that time, because that would mean discarding one of his main means of communication. It simply meant that the more information he could gather about the disorder, the more he'd have to discuss in his following sessions and the more confidence he'd gain. Knowing he wasn't alone on his journey also gave him a better idea of what he could do to help himself and also gave him a better understanding of what might be expected of him. Neal realised he was at his emotional worst when he wanted it all at once, so he focused on smaller goals to push himself forward. This meant one step at a time, one day at a time, etc.

Other tools he used were: keeping a journal and reading it monthly, writing novels to keep his mind active, crossword puzzles and art. Whenever he wrote, in journals, his books, or did crossword puzzles, it was only after Neal came out of his 'Haze', and even then, in limited times when his mind was feeling clear enough to do so.

Neal also had to deal with horrific night terrors and after waking from one he would first do his breathing exercises to calm himself down. To relax further, he'd lie there and imagine looking out a window on a rainy day, which had always had a calming effect on him.

PATTERNS FOUND WERE LESSONS LEARNED

One of Neal's biggest issues that became clearer to him as time went on was that he'd created self-doubt about how good he was as a counsellor because of what had happened to him. He later realised it wasn't weakness that had created his trauma. Once his capacity to think clearly, through all that happened, had returned, he came to the conclusion that most people given the same circumstances might have fallen into the disorder much quicker. He also realised that all people react differently, due to their varying personalities and the trauma that created the disorder initially.

Patterns of self-blame and self-belief had come to fruition over time. Cathie could also see the effect it was having. Knowing his inquisitive mind, she said to him, "You can blame yourself if you want, but I'd suggest you should just examine the circumstances. That's the only way you'll find the truth." To Neal, this became a challenge and he began to look at the past events and the help he received in detail over the six-month period leading up to his disorder. Eventually, patterns began to appear, and he came to the realisation that this was not his fault. By doing what Cathie did, she responded in a way that didn't push her opinion on Neal but made him curious enough to seek out his own answers.

Note: Set up a challenge so a person can't help but seek out the answer.

Things didn't happen overnight for Neal and there were setbacks. Through it all, he began regaining some of his cognitive clarity. He reached the point where he could research his own symptoms and log when, where and how symptoms appeared and what his reactions were. Neal sought out the patterns that related to the triggers and how those triggers related to his flashbacks and anxiety attacks. He also went searching for sounds, objects, smells and anything else that would coincide with what he'd witnessed or heard in his work as a counsellor. When he'd eventually heard one of these sounds, or smelt or seen something that triggered a flashback or an anxiety attack, he'd keep revisiting that one thing until he could make a connection and write it in his logbook. Later he would adapt a plan to overcome it.

Neal advises others not to do this unless both they and their specialist feel it's safe to do so. He continually reminds them, over and over, that what he did, didn't happen overnight. It took long periods of time with breaks in between to regain composure and refocus. Neal often gives simple lessons to others who have PTSD, because he says that he's always found that the simplest lessons are the easiest to learn from, especially when one's cognitive process is temporarily impaired. He also believes that lessons are most easily learned when you acknowledge and respect what others do right and help them work on where they feel they went wrong.

People say, "Hindsight is a wonderful thing." Neal has his own spin on this saying: "Hindsight is a wonderful thing, but only if you learn from it and use it in the future." There are many lessons to be learned in this book from both Neal and Cathie, but it's important to remember that this is based on their journey and not your own. There will always be variables in everyone's personal stories. Some of these lessons may be repeated in different scenarios throughout the book, so those reading it can grasp the meaning of what's being said, not because Neal and Cathie see you as stupid; it's because they know within themselves, when someone is going through a traumatic event, whether it be the person with the disorder or the carer, it's seriously difficult to comprehend many things as the level of anxiety is overriding their logic and making it hard to think clearly. Even a professor may find they can't focus clearly after a life-threatening event or trauma, something to remember when you're feeling inferior to others. Here's a very important lesson that both Cathie and Neal learned in the very early stages of Neal's chronic PTSD;

DON'T TRY TO FIX THE SITUATION TOO QUICKLY

Neal continues to remind us how he desperately wanted everything to immediately go back to his old normality and the harder he tried, the more frustrated he became, making his condition worse. Cathie reminds us how she wanted to fix the situation for Neal, but the more she tried, the more it seemed to aggravate him. How did that change? Both realised that what they were doing wasn't working, so they stopped and focused on other things. No, they weren't avoiding the issues; they were just taking a step back and refocusing. Cathie backed off, knowing she couldn't fix his problem on her own and sought help through other means - getting him to a doctor. Neal realised he couldn't do it on his own and took Cathie's advice and saw a doctor.

Note: No one in this world can do everything on their own; only the smart ones know *when* to ask for help.

As Neal progressed, he'd continue to jot down things in his journal and review it at the end of each month. This review was to see if there were any negative or positive results coming from certain techniques he'd used during the past month, as he worked through each issue, as it had arisen. One particular thing he'd found was writing. Writing distracted him from the stress and his over-focusing on returning to the career he'd lost.

With each small step forward, Neal would reward himself and Cathie with a breakfast or a lunch out, in a quiet spot where he felt comfortable.

As time went on, Neal began to write more and more and it had become an amazing pastime for him. He'd read Sherlock Holmes books throughout his life and he'd always wanted to write his own murder mystery, and about what had happened to him. In writing he found it inadvertently helped him fulfill that dream.

Cathie always had an interest in antiques and later began going to markets and setting up her own stall. She'd sell her antiques there, which had not only become a pleasant pastime and distraction for her but also brought Neal out of the house and he'd take his laptop with him to write while he was there.

He'd often find himself lost in the adventures of his fictional super sleuth, Sebastian Cork, a world-renowned psychologist who turned his career into solving crimes. Neal was still going through hell with his condition, but writing this series of books lifted a huge load off him. That burden had been holding him back for so long and it would have continued to do so, if he hadn't shifted his focus from his old normality. Neal learned to acknowledge the condition he had. He also learned that his PTSD would not go away as quickly as it had come, and if he wanted to learn from it, he couldn't rush or force his way through the condition. In reality it just doesn't work that way.

Note: When trying to remember something, it's often easier not to force the memory but deliberately forget it, then later it may suddenly reappear.

As you'll see throughout this book, Neal has a way of putting things into scenarios and/or hypotheticals to make it easier to comprehend. He described it this way: "If you're out running and a brick wall has been built across your everyday running track, you're not going to try and run through it, get knocked down, and then get up and do it over and over again, are you?"

We know we can't have that piece of path back, so the smart thing to do is look for other alternatives where we can still run. No, it won't be the same, but like anything else, we'll adjust and move on.

Neal said as he was reflecting back on the initial stages of his chronic PTSD, he had very little idea of most things, let alone the impact it had on his wife Cathie at that time. Cathie had to keep working for a short while to keep them financially secure, but would call in on the hour to ensure Neal hadn't done anything silly to himself. Eventually, Cathie had a minor stroke and gave up her career as a counsellor to become Neal's full-time carer. It wasn't until Neal started to emerge from the first phase of his disorder that he began to see the toll it had taken on his wife.

Both Neal and Cathie barely scraped their way out of the 'Haze' in one united piece. Their love for each other kept hope alive until that breakthrough came. Although many of his symptoms remained, once the 'Haze' finally lifted, Neal found himself capable of a small amount of focus and some intermittent clear thought, which was all he needed to begin to sort out strategies that would help him with the remaining symptoms and more importantly, to take a load off Cathie.

He strongly believed and still believes that involving himself in any research is a form of distraction. With the disorder he had, any distraction was a good one. At the same time, his research inevitably helped him regain his confidence and kept him moving consistently forward.

Note: Don't focus on who you were; focus on who you can be.

After the 'Haze' both Neal and Cathie had to put most of their negative thoughts on hold, especially Neal, as he now had clearer thinking and less emotion overriding his thoughts. He also knew that to move forward it was imperative to focus on the positives. Cathie had her negative thoughts on hold for most of the time and continued to maintain her positive outlook throughout their journey. The way Neal went about it was as soon as the negative thoughts entered his head, he'd question himself as to why he was giving any credence to some random negative thought.

Both Neal and Cathie believe that if your mind is strong enough to think negative thoughts, then it also has the capability to replace them with positive ones. This takes practice, but after time it'll become habitual in the same way the negative has.

Setting strategies is how we achieve our goals and each goal we achieve leads us to the next bigger one, but this takes patience and persistence. Yes, we'll often come across obstacles along the way and have small setbacks. These encourage us to find new strategies to achieve our goals. This is why patience and persistence are so important to our journey forward.

FREQUENTLY ASKED QUESTIONS

QUESTIONS MOST ASKED OF CATHIE

QUESTION - What do you believe was one of the most significant things you did to help Neal move forward?

ANSWER - After the first two years of Neal's chronic PTSD, I'd grown used to Neal depending on me for many things. In fact, he'd become so dependent that his dependency became part of my very own identity. I'd drive him everywhere, I'd sit with him at appointments, I'd ask him if he was alright, look for things for him - anything and everything he required, I'd make sure I'd do the best I could to get it. It was difficult at first, but then it became habitual and some things I'd even look forward to doing. Prior to Neal's condition, whenever I'd been down in the dumps or needed someone to help me through any difficult situation, Neal was always there for me and wouldn't think twice about doing what he could to help me out. So now I felt it was my turn to do the same for him.

As I said, this disorder had been going on for a couple of years, where he'd not wanted to communicate or participate in much at all. He had some good moments, but they were few and far between his withdrawals and quiet moods.

Then something changed within him. Don't get me wrong, he was still having the most horrific nightmares, flashbacks and anxiety attacks. All of a sudden he began pushing small boundaries and I'd say to him, "Do you think you should be doing that?" or, "Leave that, I'll get it for you!" until one day Neal got frustrated and angry and said to me, "How can I ever get back to normality if you continue to nurture me?" and then he walked away and slammed the door. I was stunned by the way he berated me, and I just sat down and went numb. This just wasn't the norm for him! A few minutes later Neal came back out and apologised for the way he had reacted and continued on to say,

"Cathie, I love you with all my heart and I'll be forever grateful for everything you've done for me when others would have walked away. I don't ever want you to think I don't appreciate it or you, but lately I've been feeling more aware than I have for a long time and it'd help me if you ease up on your nurturing; I really feel it's time for me to start doing more for myself." Then he looked at me with a weird grin and said, "You don't have to stop completely though!" I just nodded my head and jokingly said, "No, one in, all in!" and we both laughed.

From that day forward, I backed off from the nurturing and made myself aware by listening to his words and the tone of his voice. I stopped using my own interpretation of what I thought he said. If I was unsure, I'd ask him. I also realised that I had to try to talk in the tones I used when Neal was in his original normality and not use the nurturing one. Even though the way he spoke was harsh, which was something I'd rarely seen in him, I also realised he was right and if he hadn't made it clear, I don't think I'd have realised the dramatic change that had not only come over Neal since the beginning of his traumas but also how dramatic the change was in me. It was definitely a memorable day for both of us, because after it we both set off to regain the parts of us that had been lost in the 'Haze'. The impact was so great, neither of us had any intention of looking back.

Don't get me wrong, the path ahead wasn't an easy one to follow. We both made many adjustments along the way, but it was a path out of a very dark forest and we could see a glimmer of light, way, way up ahead.

Note: Constructive communication contributes to unity. Unity means you're no longer alone on your journey to recovery.

QUESTION - What changes did you need to make for it to work?

ANSWER - Firstly, Neal was in such a bad state, I gave up my counselling career to be closer to home to ensure his safety. Secondly, as a counsellor I'd worked with many PTSD clients before, but Neal being my husband placed me in uncharted waters. One thing I do know is it gave me an amazing insight and understanding into the realities of what, not only, a person with chronic PTSD goes through, but also carers and family members as well. I needed to get Neal professional help and that wasn't easy, but I knew it was necessary. He was referred by his doctor to the most wonderful psychiatrist initially and this helped him enormously. I think what hurt me most in the early stages of his disorder was seeing the enormous change in Neal's personality. I felt like Neal had gone off to work one day and someone else had borrowed his body when he came home. The most frightening aspect of all this was that it seemed like this new character had become embedded. To witness such a dramatic change in the personality of someone you love, and seeing him battle with it, while being affected by things that would never bother him before became not only confusing and frightening to him, but to me as well.

There were so many lessons for me to learn; what to do, but more importantly, what not to do when dealing with his chronic PTSD.

Even though Neal's hearing is far from perfect, when he finally pushed himself to go places, like large shopping centres and among a crowd, or us talking in a coffee shop, his PTSD would kick in and his hearing became hyper-sensitive and the noise became overwhelming for him. All of a sudden he'd become anxious and very pale and he'd often ask, "Why are you speaking louder than you usually do?" I'd reply, "I didn't think I was." So, whenever we were out at markets, shopping centres or among crowds, I'd try to keep my voice at a lower level.

Recently, we were discussing this particular issue and he explained he'd given it a lot of thought and the only thing he could compare it with was someone with an Inferiority Complex. He told me he'd felt insecure and inadequate when around strangers and he continued on to say that he felt he was being judged and that speaking louder than normal would draw people's attention to us. Even from a counsellor's perspective and considering that it's been a thirteen-year journey to recovery, I still find it hard to know how he overcame such a complex psychological disorder.

The other thing I found difficult to do at times was remain patient for the first two years of our journey. Neal had made little to no real moves forward, he just seemed to be drifting in and out of depression, anxiety, mood swings, horrific nightmares and flashbacks.

The only thing that seemed to help him was his writing. He was a lover of Sherlock Holmes stories in his youth and always wanted his very own super sleuth, so he started writing one. During the first book, it was a slow hard slog and he'd get frustrated with himself because he couldn't think clearly all of the time and he'd have to take intermittent breaks from his writing when he really didn't want to. He explained later that there was always something, whenever he'd have a flow of storyline happening and a trigger would occur, turning his emotions upside down and making him give up until he was ready to come back to it. By then some of the things he had in his head to write had completely gone, leaving him to reconsider where to go next within the next stages of the book. I could see how bad the flashbacks were at times when he'd try to hide the tears running down his face. Neal told me that even though writing was extremely hard at first, it slowly became more manageable and it also helped his cognitive thinking. Later it got to the point where the words and stories started to flow and he's now written five books in the series, the last one yet to be published.

Giving Neal his personal space was another must, but also difficult while living under the same roof twenty-four-seven.

As I said, there were times when Neal would tear up anytime, anywhere. We could be watching a show or just having dinner and he'd get up and walk away. Most times he'd go to the bathroom and stay there until he'd overcome his emotions. Other times he'd leave everything and just lie on the bed and keep the bedroom door closed. Initially, I'd ask him how he was, and he'd brush it off by saying he was just tired or not too well. The more I'd ask the more frustrated he'd become and would say, "I told you I'm fine!" I could see Neal needed his space, so I'd go back to watching TV or focusing on other things I wanted to do in my hobby room.

There were times when I needed my own distraction and began building model garages for the fun of it. I think we all need our own time-outs and distractions when things become too much. Taking my focus off Neal's issues for a while helped me to continue helping him and often he'd find himself in a good place and come into the hobby room and compliment me on my project. A short time later he'd leave. This was good for both of us. While I was working on one thing he'd be in the other room, either reading or writing and not just his murder mysteries but in his journal as well. Later we'd both discuss any results he'd found on what was triggering his flashbacks and what new techniques he was using to overcome many of his presenting issues.

I guess the other thing I did to help him was set certain rules on how far he should push his own boundaries during his recovery stage. At no point did I make demands on what he should or shouldn't do, but I would use questions like: "Do you feel that may be pushing it a little too far?" Or, "How will that work with the other things you're doing?" Or, "Do you feel ready for that yet and what's your plan?" Asking the questions was just the beginning, as we'd then discuss the 'Pros and Cons' and Neal would then explain how he'd go about this new idea, or he'd back off until he thought it through further.

Even for someone without PTSD, it can become uncomfortable when meeting others for the first time or at a party or a meeting where there are people you already know. Even though Neal is coping with his disorder exceptionally well now, he still uses breathing exercises whenever anxiety begins raising its ugly head. Because of the work Neal has done over such a long period of time, he rarely looks uncomfortable when doing presentations or at meetings of any kind.

There were many things that helped Neal throughout his journey. The one he used most was to find the right distraction for the right moment and to use them continually until they became habitual. This way they'd kick in by themselves whenever they were most needed.

The one thing many people don't know about Neal is he's ambidextrous and he seems to be capable of doing whatever his passions are. He's an excellent artist, he writes books, he's a very good sportsman. He's played cricket, indoor cricket, football and basketball grand finals.

He doesn't only have a practical mind which he uses to keep things down to earth. He can also think outside the square with his creative thinking. Whenever he has a problem, he'll often work at it until he overcomes it. Not bad for someone who left school at fourteen to stack bricks and then went back to school later to become an excellent counsellor. His determination, combined with his eagerness to learn, was one of the vital assets he needed to overcome the majority of issues of his chronic PTSD. How he got through the first horrific two years of his disorder can only be put down to his dogged determination until his cognitive clarity finally kicked in.

Something that really helped me through this sometimes hellish journey was allowing my mind to separate my work as his carer from my life as his wife who needed her own time-outs. Doing this helped me to continue helping him, and I stopped feeling ashamed of not being enough or doing enough, which made me exactly enough for both of us.

Note: A carer is allowed to keep their identity and should never feel ashamed of doing so.

QUESTION - Being a counsellor, why didn't you see the initial signs?

ANSWER - There's no easy answer for this one and when we both sat down and talked about it, we came to what we believe would have contributed to missing the signs. Firstly, Neal and I worked at the coal mines as counsellors with individual clients, couples and were also called to attend critical incidents on-site, twenty-four-seven. The two mines Neal worked at were long distances away, one was approximately an hour and a half away and the other, about an hour from our home.

Neal would go to the first mine site and counsel. Sometimes he was also required to counsel miners in their homes, both in the morning and afternoon. Later Neal would go to the camp and counsel again with workers who'd see him not only before dinner but after as well. He would stay at the camp overnight and then travel across to the second mine and do the same there again. Neal would then leave for home after his morning of counselling. He was also counselling in two other towns: one was only forty-five minutes from where we live, and the other about an hour and a half away. There Neal counselled at an aluminum smelter, the port offices and the offices of the power station.

The other forty-five-minute drive was working in an office counselling. Neal was also on call twenty-four-seven to attend any critical incidents that required him for counselling. Within his last six months of counselling, he attended approximately eleven critical incidents on-site when he finally broke down with chronic PTSD.

My role as a counsellor was very similar to Neal's, so as you can see a lot of the time we were like ships passing in the night and when we finally caught up, with all the travelling, stay-overs and counselling, we'd both roll home exhausted and talked-out. This made it very difficult to look for, or even see, signs from him.

Things began unraveling after all the critical incidents he'd attended. Then one day, out of the blue, he came home from one of the mines and said, "I just can't do this anymore!" and broke down and wept, something I'd never seen in twenty years of our relationship. I knew then, just how bad things were, and I got him to a doctor as soon as I could.

Note: We can't blame ourselves for what's happened to others if it wasn't our fault. All we can do is try to help them when it occurs.

QUESTION - Summarising all you have been through as a carer, what would you say was the most difficult part of your journey and what was the most rewarding?

ANSWER - The most difficult part of my journey was witnessing the loss of Neal to chronic PTSD! Seeing someone who was the most sensible and logical person I'd ever met in my life, lose all sense of purpose and not be capable of making simple decisions and relying on me for appointments and everyday life, was absolutely heartbreaking. The other hard part was that Neal had asked me to finish off sessions with a few of the clients he was concerned about at the mines. The reason this worried me was because of the state he was in, so I felt it necessary to ring home every hour to ensure he was still ok!

Neal told me he wouldn't do anything stupid, because of his faith and his love for me, but seeing him the way he was and knowing he was home by himself, was a constant worry.

As soon as I'd done what he asked, I finished at the mines. Knowing that there were some major bills coming in, I got a job closer to home, that way I could come home at night and not worry about being called out to any critical incidents.

Unfortunately, the stress of it all must have been a little too much for me as well and within a year, I had a minor stroke at work (fortunately, leaving no side effects). It made me realise something Neal had constantly said throughout our lives together whenever I'd felt down: "If you don't look after yourself, how can you look after anyone else?" So, it was then and there that I saw the stroke as a warning sign and decided to give up my career and become Neal's full-time carer.

I think the most rewarding part of my journey was learning new ways of interacting with Neal to help him move forward, being by his side and watching the advances he made. It turned out to be one of the most difficult yet also amazing journeys I'd ever been on.

I used to often say to people, “I’d love to have my old Neal back.” It wasn’t that I loved him any less, it's just that I’d missed some of his quirky ways and his wonderful sense of humour. One day he overheard me and later said when we were alone, “Please don’t say, ‘I’d love to have my old Neal back’. It makes me feel like I’m not getting anywhere and that you think less of me.” Although nothing had changed with my deep feelings for my husband and what I’d said wasn’t meant in the context he’d taken it, I could also see how it could and had hurt him. From that day on, I never said it again. Even though I felt sad that I hurt him, I also felt elated by his step forward in communicating his feelings to me in a positive manner. That day was a huge turning point in our interactions. It was evident that Neal’s awareness of how to approach his conversations with Cathie was returning.

I don’t think people realise how important communication within a relationship truly is, until it’s lost. Trust me: it’s even more important in a relationship when PTSD is involved. That day taught me that it was time for another change in approach and in order to move further forward, I'd need to begin paying more attention to how far his self-awareness had actually advanced by trying to get him to do a little more, without pushing him too far. So I opened a market stall and sold small antiques. Don't get me wrong, this wasn't only for Neal; it also got me out of the house and away from the solitary life we'd both been individually living.

At first, Neal would take his laptop to avoid looking at people who'd pass by or stop and spend money. Initially, he seemed on edge, but the more times we went, the more relaxed he'd get, just spending his time writing his murder mystery books and glancing up to look around every now and then. If there was too big a crowd or if anxiety attacks and flashbacks were prevalent, he'd bury his head into the computer and that kept him distracted for long periods of time. More and more his confidence grew with each Sunday we spent at the market. I would deliberately walk away from the stall bit by bit and go over to another stallholder to talk, while keeping an eye on him to see how he was handling it. Then one day it happened. I watched him nervously put down his laptop and talk to a customer. I was ecstatic, knowing that what I'd done was actually helping him push forward, but I also knew that without his determination and his want to push through almost impossible barriers, we couldn't have done it without both of us working as a team.

Note: We can't help others if we're not ok ourselves.

QUESTION - If you were giving advice to a carer or family member, Cathie, what helpful hints would you give them?

ANSWER - First of all, if it were the initial stages of PTSD, I feel it's important to help the person you're caring for feel safe. Don't over-empathise by talking about what they've just been through. Instead, keep a close eye on their behaviour. Let them know you're there for them and ask them if there's anything they need. If they go quiet, sit quietly with them. Then later, encourage them to seek medical advice. If things become too much for you, call for medical help.

Don't assume too much about their behaviour. Whether they seem over the top or insist they're fine, get them to a doctor, who will examine them and decide if further treatment is needed. Once the diagnosis is made and is confirmed that they have PTSD, talk to the doctor and find out what further action needs to be taken.

A little later when Neal began to see the psychologist, I spent a lot of time observing Neal and reading up on PTSD as a refresher, which actually gave me some good insight into the disorder. Anyone who hasn't studied mental health can Google PTSD to get a better understanding of the disorder. However, any further practice should be done by those who are qualified. Without meaning to, people can underestimate the intensity of what the sufferer endures, as much of it is bottled up inside. So, if you encourage the sufferer to push too hard initially, trying to make them do things they're not yet capable of, then it can actually set them back.

Neal once said to me, "People have to realise that if a sprinter were to tear a muscle on the running track, the trainer wouldn't make them get up and run another lap. Either way, it wouldn't be possible. So just because a PTSD injury can't be seen, it doesn't mean it isn't there. If a person is pushed to get over it too quickly, there's a chance their recovery could be set back, as it would with the runner."

There were long periods of time when Neal wouldn't communicate at all. At one stage, I reminded him that he had always been there for me when I needed him and that I'd like to be there for him, if he would let me. Then I left it at that so he could think about it. After a while, Neal came out and explained what was troubling him as best he could.

Most importantly, make sure you take care of yourself. You can't help someone else if you're not ok.

QUESTIONS MOST ASKED OF NEAL

QUESTION - When you were in what you called the 'Haze', what was it like, and what did you do to get through it?

ANSWER - For close to two years, I had no idea what to do. My emotions had taken full control of my logical thinking. I wanted to go back to work, but I knew I couldn't, as I didn't feel safe enough to leave the house. I wanted to be normal again but my emotions and mental capacity to think things through were all over the place. I was frustrated, angry and scared all at the same time. I had enormous trouble communicating without displaying verbal aggression, so I'd keep to myself and avoid speaking to anyone. I was having horrific nightmares and flashbacks, along with very little sleep. Something would trigger me, and I'd break into tears and tremble. In reality, I was locked out of my previous life, and a new and horrific one had taken over.

Initially, I was on medication for a short while. I found that the meds prescribed to treat my stress and anxiety also affected my receptors in the brain, which impacted whatever clear-thinking I had left. Their effect at the beginning was just what was required, but after a while, I felt that I needed to see if I could manage my condition on my own without them. It was difficult at first, but I got through the process. One of the first things I changed after coming off medication was my push to get back to my old normality and begin rebuilding a new one.

During this time I began writing murder mysteries. I would take my laptop wherever we'd go as a distraction and when at home, I'd use art in a similar fashion when things weren't too bad. The other thing I did was further research about PTSD, but only in short intervals so I wouldn't become overwhelmed. Each time I focused on something different from my old normality, a little more of it would return, in the form of clear-thinking. When I came to the realisation that the harder I pushed to reclaim the things I wanted from my previous normality, the opposite happened. It only exacerbated the problem, overloading already pent-up emotions. This chain reaction would override most logical thinking and blur the strategies that might otherwise have helped me overcome presenting issues.

Note: Sometimes retreat is the best form of attack.

QUESTION - What do you feel are good distractions to initially help people through their anxiety attacks and/or flashbacks?

ANSWER - I don't believe there's a definitive answer that covers every case. Most individuals with the disorder will have their own individual traumas and their own individual personality so they may have to devise their own distractions or adjust existing techniques to suit their own needs.

Some of the things I did during anxiety attacks, flashbacks and even nightmares were these: I'd count my fingers and thumb on one hand and then swap to the other and keep doing it until I reached fifty. I've found that with most distractions that I used, they helped my conscious mind take back control by overriding negative subconscious thoughts that were triggered by a reminder of a past trauma. I'd also go through the alphabet and name an animal for each letter for example: aardvark, bear, cat etc. It didn't have to be just animals; it could be any subject: types of dogs or cats, countries, fish or whatever subject you're comfortable with. Also, I'd sing a song in my head; one that reminded me of a good time I once had. If I was in a busy shopping centre, I'd look around for a certain colour or object, count how many people were smiling or find a certain style of clothing.

We have a lake near our home, so I'd walk around the lake and try to observe all the things around me like birds, trees, plants and water.

I would put headphones on when needed and have soothing song tracks that I'd enjoy.

Sit down and read: I'd often find that no matter where I was, reading would take my mind on a journey and make me feel at ease.

The thing that I feel helped most was writing a journal. I'd jot down where and when I had the anxiety attack or flashback, what I heard or saw at that time, what was happening around me and then try to identify what I thought may have been the trigger. I'd continue to do this until I could see a pattern emerging and then work on overcoming what it was that was triggering me. The interesting thing about this was, that even though it was done during the anxiety attack, it also worked as a distraction by moving my focus to the solution and not the problem itself.

Note: Just hunting for answers can sometimes be the answer, by it becoming a distraction to the overriding problem.

QUESTION - What do you believe was one of the biggest turning points in creating change in the way you saw PTSD, and how did you make that happen?

ANSWER - Training my brain to accept PTSD as my competitor and not my master. It's like when you have a negative thought about someone, and then you correct that thought by re-engaging your brain to question that impulse; at that very moment you're competing with that irresponsible thought and you're overturning a verdict because it lacks proof.

So this is how I used this technique: when cockatoos would fly over our house, I'd have anxiety attacks; their noise was a reminder of a past trauma and would create a flashback to that time. So I'd immediately slow my breathing while looking around and reminding myself that I was in a comfortable room, in the here-and-now, and that time had passed. I'd then focus on objects within the room itself. I used the exact same technique with my horrific nightmares.

The more often I competed with my negative thinking, the more embedded my positive thoughts became and would automatically kick in bringing me back to some sort of normality.

Note: When competing, determination often comes naturally - it doesn't have to be forced, it is a calm sense of focus.

QUESTION - What simple things can I do to help myself through my own PTSD?

ANSWER - Live one day at a time. Don't over-think things initially and work to occupy your mind with simple tasks like exercise, reading, walking, art, routine small jobs around the house, or whatever it is that you feel will keep your mind busy without too much stress or over-thinking. Frustration comes from over-thinking and trying to problem-solve when your brain needs a break from exactly that. So continuing to think about these things can create more issues.

I'm sure you wouldn't try doing sprints with trauma from a torn muscle, which was caused by over-exertion; you'd wait for it to heal first. Well, your brain's no different; it also needs a break from overuse when it's had a trauma.

Distraction is the key initially; it helps us focus on other things until we're ready to accept that what's happened is over and those recurring issues that come back to haunt us are no longer in our here-and-now. By using distraction, it becomes a habitual tool to get us through the roughest parts of our journey and to help overcome many of the fears that rise up from our subconscious mind.

One example I use is that once I'd regained enough confidence to enter large shopping complexes, I'd often be overwhelmed by anxiety and my immediate response was flight, but the thoughts that I'd implanted over and over into my head kept reminding me that PTSD is my competitor and not my master, so I'd take my car keys from my pocket and look at them and then envisage places I'd travelled to, so that comforted me, while at the same time, I'd slow my breathing until the anxiety had left me.

I will continue to repeat throughout this book that none of this happens overnight and like anything else, we only get results out of something we've put the effort into and worked for.

Note: Even the simplest goals need to be practised over and over before you reach out for a larger one. So, there are simple things to do, but like everything else, they take practice before you get a result, as does anything else. Whether it's a new

job, a new hobby, a sport etc., everything in our entire lives takes practice and persistence if we want to achieve our end goals. For me PTSD was no different, we can't just want normality back - we first have to have a strategy to get it and then with help from professionals and those who care begin to work toward our first small goal at a pace that is realistic to how we're coping at that time.
Not everything always goes to plan so it's necessary to communicate with those important people in your life and brainstorm where we go from there. I also found it important when things went wrong (which they did many times) not to create my own victim. As frustrating as it was at times, take one day at a time and even if it's in your own backyard, walk it off or get a punching bag and release that pent-up energy, any exercise will help when you need to release.

QUESTION - I get so frustrated and sometimes really angry and it's difficult for me to communicate with others when I'm feeling this way, which is quite often. How did you deal with that?

ANSWER - When I used to have trouble with communication, I tried to use it wisely. I did this by explaining my feelings and needs to others when I was in my calmest state. I explained to people I was communicating with that there'd be times when it's difficult for me to express myself and that it'd be better for me to take a break and talk later when I've calmed down, but I always made sure I'd follow through with the conversation when I was able to. What I also found helped with communication (and as difficult as it may seem) was to try to maintain awareness of my own actions and feelings so that I'd know if I was beginning to feel agitated or annoyed. In this way I could either quickly act to change what was happening at that moment or pause the conversation and return to it later.

Self-awareness can make a huge difference in a conversation. Awareness of the intensity in your own voice or negative thoughts toward the other person can tell you it's time to stop. This way it doesn't get to a point where there's a lack of control over the words being spoken, but it's imperative to come back later to finish the conversation. However, if you feel you've been offended by what's been said to you, or they talk over the top of you and you feel that you can't come back to that particular issue/issues, wait until you're calm and write down your thoughts in a polite letter or email. Say how you felt when they did or said the things you felt offended by. Also, write down the things you needed to say during the conversation and how it made you feel when you couldn't say them. Try to be constructive rather than rude in the way you write it and then leave it where they can find it if you feel uncomfortable giving it to them directly. By writing your feelings and thoughts down, no one can talk over the top of you or talk down to you or ignore what you have to say, but it's very important to be constructive and not abusive. That's why I say, being calm and respectful when writing is an absolute must. When doing it this way, I'd find it very unusual for you not to be heard within the course of them reading your letter.

Note: Keeping calm is a solid base to build effective communication on.

Keeping calm can also help with preparation prior to a conversation. I found breathing exercises helped both **before** an organised conversation and **during** an unexpected conversation, when I felt a little anxious.

There were times when during conversations, I'd have mental blanks and I'd get so frustrated with myself that Cathie would sometimes think I was angry with her when I stormed off. It wasn't until later when I came back and explained what was really going on, that my storming off wasn't aimed at her but part of the disorder I was dealing with. Once she knew and understood how much these blocks heightened my emotions to an unbearable point, she'd calmly reassure me and tell me it's ok by either saying, “Do you want to take a break?” or “It’s ok, we can come back to that later.” So, expressing what we’re feeling helps others to feel more comfortable when communicating with us.

Note: Nobody knows what we’re thinking or feeling inside, so until we communicate it, we have no right to expect them to understand.

QUESTION - You wrote in your first book that people with PTSD should seek out others such as a doctor initially and then you may be referred to a psychiatrist or psychologist. After thirteen years with PTSD, do you continue to see a psychiatrist or psychologist?

ANSWER - Yes, I do, but nowhere near as often as I used to. I do still have an excellent psychologist whom I like to see to keep myself in check and discuss where I’m at. I feel it reassures me that I’m still on track and keeping myself within certain boundaries of my workload as a counsellor.

As far as my PTSD is concerned, I believe awareness has given me the advantage in recognising my conscious thinking and also keeps my subconscious thinking in check. Believe it or not, once I habitually worked to conquer the negatives of conscious thoughts, it helped me to recognise any negative thoughts emerging from my subconscious. This doesn't mean that we can overcome every issue that arises; otherwise we wouldn't be reading books like this one to learn more, and this is one of the reasons I continue to see my psychologist intermittently, so I can learn even more ways of dealing with any arising or left-over issues.

The interesting thing is, no two psychologists will be the same, as no two counsellors or psychiatrists or even people for that matter can be, but we can learn something different from each and every one of them. Many of these professionals may learn the same therapies but each will apply them in their own manner and with their own interpretations.

Note: Finding out who and what's important to you gives back some sense of self-control.

Whether we have PTSD or not, we should never be ashamed of seeking help from a mental health professional if we need one. Many of us were brought up to believe that someone having some sort of mental illness means they're completely insane and should be avoided at all costs - that's absolute rubbish.

As time goes by, there are more and more positive advancements within the mental health field and not just through medication. Some people go to psychologists or counsellors over short terms due to a stressful situation they may not be able to handle alone - this could be a death in the family, not being able to deal with a domestic or work situation or even traumas as well as just everyday stresses. What I find strange is the stigma around going to a person who works in the mental health field as they're sworn to complete confidentiality, except where there is an issue of safety to yourself or someone else. Yet most of us have no problems talking to a neighbour or an acquaintance over personal issues that may concern us. By the way, most counsellors and psychologists are encouraged by their governing organisations to have counselling supervision to promote well-being and professional development.

QUESTION - What simple reminders can I use to deal with some of the symptoms of PTSD?

ANSWER - In the initial stages of PTSD, allow professionals to have a bit more input when it comes to your condition since they'll have a better awareness and a clearer perspective than you do.
In my initial stages of chronic PTSD, it was difficult for me to think with any clarity at all. Yes, I had my moments, but in reality it was more often that my emotions were overriding my logic, and even

though I didn't want anyone telling me what I should or shouldn't do, if I hadn't heeded their advice, I might have remained lost in the world I'd initially found myself in. I resisted for a while; but in one small moment of lucidity, I eventually realised I couldn't plan this difficult escape from within, by myself. What really helped me was working on my patience; as discussed before, in the initial stages of my PTSD all I wanted was to escape, which pushed my anxiety through the roof when it didn't happen. Once I stopped pushing and used patience, I began focusing on other things and that's when my anxiety became more intermittent and my focus gained more clarity. So, patience became the key to slowing my intense push to get over PTSD and helping me to focus on the things I **could do** and not the things I **could not do** in those very early stages. Eventually, cognitive thinking made its way back in its due time and not when I wanted it to.

Often there are times when we forget something that we really want to remember and we keep trying to force ourselves to remember it but the more we stress over it, the harder it becomes to bring that memory to the surface. Later, when the stress fades, the memory somehow resurfaces with clarity.

Stress and anxiety are often a reflex action; at other times, anxiety can be fuelled by events or pure frustration. What I realised was that once I learned to calm the frustration, I was able to reduce much of my anxiety.

Help your frustration and anxiety by learning breathing techniques; it will contribute to slowing down the rapid breathing that comes with the anxiety. Then use distraction by focusing on nearby objects or things that remind you of calm, happy memories. With flashbacks, remind yourself that you're in the here-and-now and what caused your issues are in the past. With horrific nightmares, I focus on what's around me and slow my breathing.

When I have trouble getting back to sleep, I'll often focus on a place where I've felt safe in the past or play a song that'll take my mind to another time.
Note: Lessons in life are learned from two sources: experience and the words of others.

QUESTION - How did you eventually find a way out?

ANSWER - Simply put, by being consistent when using all the techniques and strategies that have been laid out in this book. Consistency in my eyes means that if you start a project, you work hard to see it through.
The hardest part was getting my cognitive thinking back at the start of this journey so I needed help to do that. Once this was done, it was up to me to continue the good work others had done, and were still doing, for me.
All the techniques and tools in this book were not just used once, but as many times as they were

needed; the only way they could become habitual was by focusing on what I needed in the here-and-now and then practicing it consistently. If I remained totally focused on the past traumas, I'd still be where I was. The longer I consistently practised, the more my cognitive thinking would improve; as it improved, I could set more goals, achieving more each time, and with every achievement my confidence grew and my anxiety lessened. All of this created a positive chain reaction that kept the momentum going steadily forward. To me, it ran parallel to the ideals I'd been using most of my life: the more you practice, train or study, the better you become at it. However, the more you force yourself to do something, the harder it becomes. This doesn't mean that you don't try; it means if it doesn't work, look for another way, and if you can't find one, talk to someone who can help guide you.

In the past, none of us have received the knowledge and/or our experience by waving a magic wand. When we encounter unfamiliar problems, we don't say "I give up, this is just too hard", if we really want to master them. What we'll normally do is talk to others who know about it or read about it or we'll train to become better at it until we begin to make progress. Once we get to this stage, we'll practise; with consistency, it eventually becomes the norm. For example: think about when we first began to write, type, cook, play sports, ride a horse, saddle it or drive a car. Weren't there times when we felt like giving up? However, the prize at the end of the lessons could make our lives so much better; therefore, we refused to throw in the towel. Well, to me, no matter how long it took, the prize at the end of my journey was much too important to miss out on. Now that I'm here, I've become aware that it's been so long since I've felt so proud about an achievement. I'm grateful to those who stood by my side throughout the journey. Note: We can never rebuild an old life, but we can incorporate parts of it when we're building the new one; both do require lessons, practice and persistence.

QUESTIONS THE AUDIENCE HAVE ASKED NEAL AND CATHIE

During and after many of the presentations, Neal and Cathie asked the audience why, as family members of people with PTSD, they hadn't sought help for themselves once they became carers?

These were some of the responses:

"Because it wasn't me who was in the accident!"

"Well, I didn't see what she saw!"

"I wasn't the one who went to war, he was!"

"I was too busy trying to look after him."

"Why would I do that? That's unfair to him?"

AFTER THOUGHTS

Due to embedded beliefs, many family carers find themselves fully focusing on those who are suffering while ignoring their own stresses.

From childhood we recognise if our siblings or parents or those we love are hurt. Our immediate focus becomes fixed on doing something that shows we care and if we as children ask for attention at an inappropriate time during someone else's illness, the possibility of being called inconsiderate can become the norm. So, as we grow, the primary focus becomes about those who are suffering and to react any other way isn't perceived as the norm and to think otherwise can often create a sense of guilt. Sadly, the guilt of considering oneself, while helping another, can then take precedence over our own welfare.

Cathie made it very clear that through her journey as a wife and carer, that she'd fallen into that trap of having her absolute focus on her husband's welfare to the point where, as he began to evolve out of his 'Haze', she never considered that looking after his issues and his well-being had been so obsessive. It had become part of her very identity and once she acknowledged this, she realised she had to regain what she'd lost herself.

POSITIVE THINKING

Neal believes strongly in patterns of behaviour, which can either be positive or negative. He goes on to say if we habitually tell ourselves how hard things are or how impossible it is and we've tried, but it doesn't and/or won't work, then we create a pattern of behaviour that can lead to creating our own victim. He felt a better alternative would be to change those negative patterns of thought into positive ones by arguing with them, for example: “I'll never become any more than I am now!” and then using an immediate response, his thought would be, “No, that's not true! If I work at it, I can do it!”

Constant reaffirmation of being capable then becomes as habitual as the negativity and eventually, the negativity begins to dwindle.

EMBEDDED BELIEFS

Someone once said to Neal, “How can you help others if you can’t look after yourself?” The reality is you can’t! This doesn’t mean you have to be heartless, far from it, nor does it mean others have to know that you’re seeking help for yourself; it just means it’s ok to not be ok!

We all have specific ways of dealing with issues and we also use some variations of those specific ways that have been implanted into us from a very young age, for example: ‘Don’t talk to strangers’, ‘Look both ways before crossing the road’, ‘Wash your hands before you eat and after going to the toilet’, ‘Put your hand up if you’re in trouble when swimming’ and the list goes on with many more that are passed down through individual families. These embedded beliefs are normally taught to us to make us aware of dangers we may face in life. We also have others that teach us how to cope with issues when an accident may occur, such as 'Wrap a tourniquet around your leg or arm to help stop bleeding', 'Put a cold compress on your head or body if it's suffered a blow, to prevent swelling.'

So, if all these and more embedded preventatives and cures are put in place to help heal us, what happens when a major trauma occurs in our lives and it doesn't fit into any categories we've learned, and we can't find a way to fix it? On top of this major trauma, our brain becomes overloaded, trying to problem-solve, but it can't because there's no data stored anywhere in our mind.

How does a person react when they've fallen deep in a crevice, trapped under a car, been shot in a hunting accident in the middle of nowhere or got lost on a hike without a compass?

Anything that affects us over time is easier to cope with because we're constantly adjusting, but when it strikes out of nowhere, initially we have no idea how to overcome it. As for the loved ones who see the result of how quickly it changes someone who has just faced a traumatic incident, unless they're in a job that deals with trauma, most of the time they're not sure how to react either.

Some outsiders may see a depressed person with PTSD and without knowing what the person with PTSD has seen or done, say things like "They're just faking it!" or "I've been through worse, they just need to get over it!" or "They're just plain nasty, no patience at all!" When judging their actions too critically, it can make the situation worse and will often agitate and aggravate the person who already has so many emotional stresses from their PTSD. It could even trigger them into becoming verbally abusive.

What makes people assume they know what someone with PTSD is going through? Have they actually taken time to consider these assumptions, or are they coming from their own embedded beliefs? Wouldn't it be more important to validate the person with the disorder's issues than to respond with negative questions, criticism or disbelief?

For example, he or she might say, "I just can't cope with this overload in my head!" Instead of telling them to stop complaining, this is where a positive response can make all the difference. Perhaps we could reply, "How would you feel if we tried to work through it together?" or "As you know what you're feeling better than I do, it would help if you could fill me in along the way; that way I can get a better understanding of what you're up against. What do you think?" At this point, the person with PTSD may feel less alone and less pushed into something they're not yet ready for. Once we begin to push someone with PTSD too early to get better, the person feels segregated and frustrated. This could cause their anxiety to rise and override their logical thinking, leading them into fight-or-flight mode. In this situation ‘fight’ rarely means physically; more times than not, it’s verbally.

Neal related the story of when he was a small boy; he recalled how he’d stayed over at his uncle and auntie’s place, who owned a dairy. On occasion, his uncle would take Neal with him on the milk run and his uncle would do this on the back of what looked like a chariot, while a Clydesdale horse would pull it along. Each time his uncle needed to deliver the bottles of milk, he’d make sure Neal was secure and then jump off the back of the cart while the horse continued plodding down the road. Unbeknownst to Neal, the horse was trained not to spook under most circumstances and also knew the roads to travel down. You can just imagine Neal as a small boy watching his uncle jump off for the first time to deliver bottles of milk, while he was left there on a moving cart and imagining all sorts of mishaps, but in reality, that old horse had done the trip hundreds of times and knew exactly what to do.

Each time Neal experienced that ride, he enjoyed it more and actually looked forward to doing it again. So many of us assume what others may be thinking and/or catastrophise about things that may go wrong.

Maybe this story is a good lesson for those who mock and/or make assumptions about other people's thoughts, when they haven't taken the time to research what's really going on and that can't be seen. We can often assume that we fully understand someone who is very close to us, but when PTSD consumes them after a trauma or a number of traumas, it's hard for us to grasp that for as long as it takes, this will no longer be the person we once knew. If we take our time to educate ourselves on what's really happening in the here-and-now, we can all get more attuned to it in a logical manner, but if we allow our emotions and negative embedded thoughts to override our logical thinking, we can't achieve the best for them or ourselves, and the mend won't come as quickly.

If we're still unsure and feeling insecure about a situation, we should definitely consider discussing the overriding issues with those who would have a better knowledge of that particular problem and get the right advice, rather than assuming everything that we believe may happen will happen.

HOW WRITING HELPED NEAL

One of the most difficult things Neal had to do throughout his journey with chronic PTSD was normalise his thoughts. Initially, it was something he couldn't do alone due to the extreme nature of his condition, which he said created a horrid haze that would cloud and confuse his normally clear and logical mind. Once the 'Haze' had eventually cleared, some of his original focus and understanding of more complex issues and problems began to restore a certain amount of self-confidence back into his life, and it was at that very point that his life and mental health began its journey back.

The very first step he took turned out to be his most important one, and that step was to normalise his PTSD by accepting it as a disorder that can happen to anyone at any time, and that he was capable of adapting to it and living with it if he just rolled up his sleeves and worked at it. At no stage did this mean giving in to it, it meant, while living with it, he'd have to look for its flaws first, and once they were found, he could find ways of working through them. So, Neal set off to do more research, while still making sure he was alert not to overdo it. He did this by pacing himself and resting when he needed to. Essentially, Neal had made his chronic PTSD his competitor rather than his master.

Neal knew and accepted that he couldn't go back to his career as a counsellor at this stage, so he considered other options that he used to enjoy doing or things he'd like to be doing at that time, things that would help him build further on his rational thinking. Once he'd established parameters on the length of time and days that would need to be set out into a reliable routine so it wouldn't overload his rational thinking, he also considered time-outs if anxiety hit or things became overwhelming for him.

After much consideration and planning, writing and painting were the two things that Neal felt would help him regain his focus and also help him to avoid overwhelming anxieties that would normally occur when he'd put too much pressure on himself to achieve. Both painting and writing were enjoyable to him, and he rarely felt pressured when doing them, but if it did put too much pressure on him, he had a plan to pull back and occupy his mind with something else, which would often be reading or research, or even kicking back and watching TV.

Once Neal had come out of the 'Haze' that he honestly thought he'd never make it through, he was still experiencing overwhelming anxiety, triggers leading to flashbacks and horrific nightmares, but as he began writing, his anxiety eased. He'd taken the exaggerated pressure of returning to work off himself by refocusing his thoughts on his stories and characters, and all of this had created a positive distraction, which in turn helped reignite his logical and creative thinking. It was like a sportsperson, gradually exercising to come back after a major injury. Writing would gently nudge his inner thoughts and thought choices in a positive manner, and when it came to working out different scenarios, it would involve his imagination when portraying individuals, characters and personalities.

Prior to writing, Neal would focus on his car keys when a flash-back or anxiety attack would hit, but now he could whisk himself away on a journey in one of his books, until the flash-backs and anxiety disappeared.

There are things we discuss repeatedly in this book, and the reason for this is it gives the reader, whether it be a carer or someone with the disorder, the opportunity to increase their focus on the important issues discussed. When Neal wanted to change negative thoughts into positive ones with repetitive reaffirmation, he'd repetitively turn his negatives into positives until it was habitual, and his attitude became a positive one. The same repetition also works with positive reaffirmations, as well as reminders of solutions and techniques, written in different scenarios and forms.

One of Neal's most repeated objectives that he'd like PTSD sufferers to focus on is the journal or logbook. He truly believed that this helped him enormously, and he still uses it to this day. How it worked: Neal always kept a notebook and pen on him wherever he went. Later, he'd copy his notes into a larger logbook after returning home with Cathie from a large shopping centre. Anytime something triggered an anxiety attack or a flashback, after it was over, he'd jot down what he was seeing and hearing at that time, so he could later reflect on what had occurred. He also kept a list of the critical incidents he'd attended and would often ponder them to find out which sound or sight was more likely to relate to the anxiety attack or flash-back. Once Neal began matching some of these up, and identifying their connection, it became easier for him to put measures in place around those types of objects or noises. The majority of those flashbacks are no longer triggered by those noises or sights. The flashbacks have also lost their impact to the point that they now come to him as just bad memories, like many other people do when reflecting on something negative from their past.

Neal's a big one for scenarios, as you may have already noticed as you've read through this book. The way he describes how he overcame these flashbacks was, once he could identify the triggers, then he could change how the trigger was tricking his brain with a lie.

So, here is how this works: in one of Neal's scenarios, imagine you've fallen on a train track and the train's heading straight for you. You hear the whistle, you try to get up, but your foot is caught, and the whistle is getting louder and louder until finally you pull your foot free and roll out of the way just in time. Now, this terrifying incident has left you traumatised, and every time you hear a kettle boil, or a child's whistle, or a car screech, you have a flashback of that day, and because that trauma was so overwhelming, you may not consciously connect the kettle whistle with the train whistle, but subconsciously it's a different matter, and all you can think about is the pure fear and image of that train coming at you. Once you finally connect the trigger to the flashback, you can then focus on how to overcome it.

When Neal began searching for, and then finding his triggers, he'd deliberately allowed himself to confront them intermittently and with long deliberate pauses, over and over again. As he explained in his first book, cockatoos would fly over his house in the morning and the noises would make him shake and bring him to tears. Once Neal had connected the screeching noise to a trauma he'd attended and helped save a life, he'd wait for the cockatoos to fly over and begin taking deep breaths in and slowly out, while repeating over and over in his mind: 'Oh, wow, the cockatoos are here.' The noise he'd heard on that traumatic day was a screeching noise similar to the cockatoos, but in reality, it wasn't the same. Once he'd worked to convince himself of that, by interrupting those false negative thoughts and then replacing them with repetitive, positive realities, those new thoughts, slowly but surely brought him back to a here-and-now reality.

Initially, Neal's thoughts had been running amok at super-speed with false perceptions of the here-and-now reality, and once he began prompting his mind with a new reality thinking process and made it habitual, his hyper-sensitive thoughts began to calm and slow down. Like any chain reaction, this then allowed him to regain more and more ability to think in a controlled way.

NEAL'S THOUGHTS ON DISTRACTION

Another tool that's been spoken about repetitively throughout this book because of the important role it played in Neal's recovery is distraction and I guess Neal looked at this in a broader sense than just through the eyes of someone with PTSD. What he's actually doing here is trying to help the reader to understand that most things we do in life are habitual and to change those habits is uncomfortable. While in reality we don't see that many of the tools Neal uses are basic and we already use them in similar ways to help us constantly, without giving them a second thought because they've been unknowingly learned and practised until they've also become habitual. His thoughts on distraction are that it's bigger than most of us imagine and that we use it so often we don't even realise we're doing it.

How often do we see someone sitting alone in a café texting or watching a video? Isn't this a distraction? Are hobbies like fishing, reading, sailing or swimming, just something a person enjoys or are they also calming, positive distractions from our everyday stresses of life? So if they can be used as a calming, positive distraction to help keep us from overstressing throughout our lives, then why not focus on these to help with traumas and anxieties. Yes, trauma is on an entirely different emotional plane but if used in a constant and habitual way while employing different variations for each individual's needs, then we need to ask ourselves, what healing benefits would distraction have in calming intense emotions and traumatic memories for someone with PTSD? A child may be crying and upset so what's the first thing adults use to calm them down? A distraction of course!

There are numerous distractions a parent or adult will use when trying to calm an emotionally upset child for example: a doll or teddy, a rattle, an ice cream, a song and the list goes on and on, depending on what distraction suits each individual child. So, the same applies to someone with PTSD having an anxiety attack; they're the best judge of their own individual distraction. Neal's plan was to find his own personal distractions to use whenever anxiety would overwhelm him. He believed no journey into the unknown is an easy one and people require tools to help them along the way; they also need to plan ahead and ready themselves for the unforeseen issues that may arise out of nowhere. His other thoughts were to practise his distractions over and over again by using his imagination to take him to a safe place. He'd also use his power of observation to distract and calm him down when anxiety was overwhelming his conscious mind.

During anxiety attacks, he'd often imagine himself in a different setting or place where he felt comfortable or look around him and focus intensely on an object or colour. In large shopping centres, it wasn't easy initially, as triggers would keep arising out of nowhere, but once Cathie had found a coffee shop that Neal felt safe and comfortable with, they'd use the same pathway there each time.

This journey became habitual and the more Neal did it, the more comfortable he became and over time he also began to see the triggers that brought on his anxiety, which had then become more recognisable. He recalls one of the triggers being screaming children as they walked past the play area and he also realised through this that whenever he was out, all noises seemed to amplify many times louder than they would in the comfort of his own home. There were times that he'd ask Cathie to keep her voice down because he felt people were looking at them, but in reality, she was just speaking as she normally would. After talking with many other sufferers of this disorder, he found they had felt the same way, so he studied this unusual symptom further and found the cause: Hyperacusis (noise sensitivity).

During these experiences while out, Cathie would continue to keep a close eye on Neal. She said she'd continued to watch his facial expressions and body language, to make sure he wasn't overdoing things and would sometimes use a distraction with him by asking what he was going to have for breakfast there, or if he saw what was on display at a shop they passed. She made the point that if done sparingly, a carer can also help the person with PTSD with distractions as well, but if overdone, their sensitive condition will pick up on what you're doing and in Neal's own words, "It can make you feel inferior or less capable of dealing with your own issues, due to the sensitive nature of your condition."

From Neal's experience as a counsellor, he'd found the clients he'd worked with prior to his own PTSD weren't dangerous at all, and if there ever was a display of annoyance, it often came from the frustration they were experiencing in the very early stages of their disorder. He began to fully understand why and that was due to his own personal experience.

Neal has constantly said that the most difficult experiences came within the very first stage of his disorder, which he called the 'Haze'. Initially when clients came to him and told him how hard it was to explain what they were feeling and that there was nothing like it, Neal would then work around the other issues they had and what they could do to overcome them, but until he was struck down with chronic PTSD himself, he openly admitted that he could only give vague examples of what it felt like but then went on to stress that no one will ever know the extremities of this condition until they actually have a lived experience like those who have been through it. He once tried to explain it like this, "Every single thing about it was horrific. Not knowing how to escape something that wouldn't allow you to think clearly, or a maze in your mind that would make you think you've found your way out, and then you'd realise you were back at the start of the maze again. You'd constantly crave your free thinking to return like a smoker craves a cigarette when he has none and no money to buy them. Your frustration becomes like a person who's inebriated and wants to drive their car home, even though they can barely walk, let alone drive, and the drunken annoyance and frustration emerges from normally responsible people who are now lacking in clear thought with the abrupt loss of their own self-image and pride!"

Neal makes it clear that the list of these barely describable hypothetical examples is only a skerrick of the symptoms. Furthermore, he added a similarity to the deepest depression you could imagine with constant sobbing and dissociation to frustration and extreme anxiety. The point he was trying to make was this: if you were able to place his extreme symptoms under a magnifying glass, it would begin with the loss of his focus and awareness to make clear and concise judgements and decisions, amongst all that was frustration, anxiety, shame and embarrassment. Neal said all he could think about was that he wanted to go back to work; he needed to get over all of what he was going through and would constantly remind himself, 'I'm a bloody counsellor, what the heck is wrong with me? Why do people look at me like that? Why am I crying like a baby for no real reason at all?'

So, not being able to control what used to be his calculated, clear and focused thinking, totally created an enormous fear, frustration and anger within him and once he began convincing himself it may never go away and he may never return to his original normality, his enormous fear turned into uncontrollable anxiety.

Scientists would perhaps use similar words to this, 'When PTSD is triggered by the reminder of a traumatic event, the person on the receiving end of that trigger loses their access to their prefrontal cortex, which is the holder and bearer of the brain's rational decision-making.' Neal's way of putting it is simply this, "My emotions and irrational thinking are temporarily overriding my clear and rational thinking."

CATHIE'S THOUGHTS ON FAMILY MEMBERS AND FRIENDS OF THOSE WITH THE DISORDER

Throughout this book, Cathie emphasises that when someone you love is going through what Neal was experiencing with his disorder, you feel helpless and you also feel some of their emotional pain. She went on to clarify that we should never, ever assume we feel it all or consider their emotional pain isn't as bad as it seems.

Cathie made this vital point, that when Neal did finally begin to communicate clearly, even she was astonished at some of the things he'd told her and even now can't come close to imagining how he's come as far as he actually has. Cathie continues to make the point of how tough a journey it has been for both of them, along with believing the lessons they've received from their journey were an invaluable source of information for both those with the disorder and their loved ones and carers. Just knowing that they've been through one of the hardest journeys of their lives and are now back counselling, doing presentations and consulting with companies and organisations, helps others understand that if you're prepared to work through issues with patience and love, there can be light at the end of the darkest tunnel.

Cathie believes if you want a quick fix, don't always expect it.

Some people are resilient when it comes to trauma leading to PTSD and get over it much quicker, but many don't, and it takes time and patience to help them on their journey to recovery.

Cathie also found when caring for Neal that the best way to get positive outcomes was by how she connected and communicated with him. It came through less communication and more listening and then responding with interest, while at the same time **not** being patronising or treating him like a victim. Simply put, it was about keeping as much normality as possible, while not pushing conversations with Neal, but allowing him to lead the way and then for her to remain alert to what he said, without focusing on what her next question or statement will be. If Cathie had butted in before he finished speaking, she would have found that Neal clammed up and even walked off in a huff. It's already incredibly difficult and frustrating for someone with PTSD to communicate their feelings, so if she had jumped in before he'd finished, he'd shut down all communication, as it was so easy for him to lose his train of thought.

Yes, both their journeys were difficult and each day presented new challenges, but there were also good days and amazing feelings of achievement as each of them overcame their very own roadblocks and learned vital lessons that would give them a grateful sense of warmth and satisfaction when they later saw the great results of their work with others. As one journey ended and another began, they then knew that those thirteen years hadn't been wasted and that God had his own plans for them.

MENTAL EXERCISES NEAL USED DURING TIMES OF RATIONALITY

Neal would use repetition to change his thought process during flashbacks and/or night terrors. He'd do this with reminders that he was in the here-and-now and that what happened is like other bad memories of the past; it's gone and no longer exists. He'd wake up in the mornings focused on the day ahead and when people asked him how he was, he'd tell them he woke up breathing; so he'd had a great start to his day. How about you?

Don't have expectations, good or bad. It is better to set goals with smaller rewards that lead to a larger goal with a larger reward and just keep working towards them inch by inch. There may be setbacks along the way and if we're expecting to get there without them, then we can end up giving up on our final target.

Argue with habitual negative thoughts and turn them into positive ones. Neal reiterates that what he found most times throughout his journey is that whenever he felt he was on track for positive outcomes, his brain would look for negatives like: **'What if this happens?'**, **'I'm not sure I'll be able to do that!'**, and **'I can't see this ever ending!'** How about: **'No one really cares!'** and **'No one understands!'** When he took the positives on board, he began debating those negatives, until it became habitual and eventually overrode them. The more he did it, the more often the positive thoughts became the norm. This doesn't mean that we shouldn't think through our thoughts or use common sense when it comes to setting goals or dismissing exaggerated outcomes. It just means that when facing unrealistic negatives in our heads, we should question their integrity.

Here's how he would focus on and deal with the above negatives in his head: let's look at this first negative: **'What if this happens?'** To Neal, this could have either become a negative block for further goals, or he could have turned it into, 'Mmm, never thought of that, I'll have to put a plan in place in preparation for it. Glad I thought about that!' A more important point to consider would be: 'Well, it hasn't happened yet and I need to focus on one day at a time.'

First, the subject is defined and creates a positive aspect he can work with, so what seemed like a negative turns into a positive.

Let's keep going: **'I'm not sure I'll be able to do that!'**

With a statement like this one, Neal would be looking for the reasons why he'd initially made it and ask himself, "Am I in a negative frame of mind and it's just something I've said to avoid attempting it?" Or, "Are there real issues blocking my move forward that I **can** work to overcome and continue on my track forward?"

Here he's examined the negative thought and created a more realistic and positive way forward.

Another is: **'I can't see this ever ending!'**

With this scenario in his mind, he'd be focusing on what he can't do that's different from what he basically can do at a later given time. Once the **'can't** 'enters into an equation, it not only eliminates what can be done in the here-and-now, but also what can be planned for our future goals. This is a lesson he'd learned from having chronic PTSD. All Neal wanted to do was go back to his dream job of counselling and the more he focused on it, the worse it got and there was no way known he could ever see PTSD ending.

The thing that changed it all was positive thinking and letting go of the **obsession** of returning to what was his normality before PTSD. After he did that and focused on a new adventure, what seemed like a 'Haze' before, slowly (when I say slowly, I literally mean slowly), his awareness began to return bit by bit, allowing him to focus on his new projects. Eventually, with some remnants of Neal's ordeals and bits and pieces that may never leave him, he could see light at the end of the tunnel, to the point that he's now counselling again.

Where once Neal would rarely go outside due to anxiety and panic attacks with flashbacks and horrific nightmares, along with a resistance to enter shopping centres, he's now doing things differently. Neal is attending meet and greets at wellness days with Cathie, while representing her business (Beyond PTSD) and also giving presentations in crowded rooms and counselling. So, please hear me when I say: there's always light at the end of the tunnel. Just be patient with yourself and reshape your focus off what was, to what can be.

How about, **'No one really cares!'**

With Neal's disorder he felt so inhibited that he pushed away from others, including Cathie for a while, the one person who cared so much. Cathie gave up her career as a counsellor to become his full-time carer. There were times when Neal didn't want to talk to her because he had so much frustration, emotional pain and anger raging in his head, that he knew if he opened up with his emotions overriding his logic, he'd say things he didn't mean. So, it's very easy for Neal to imagine how frustrating it would be for carers to understand what their loved ones are going through, too.

If you have PTSD, both Neal and Cathie say to you, "Others do sincerely care about you, but sometimes they have no idea what's going on inside of you." The only way you can change this negative issue into a positive one is to focus on how and when you can communicate with them so they can get some small understanding of what you're going through and what would be the best way for them to approach it. This can be done by saying to yourselves, “As soon as I’m calm and have some awareness, I’ll work on a short amount of communication and I’ll try hard to do this in a positive manner or I’ll write you a note explaining what I’m feeling, but if and when it gets overwhelming and you want to continue, I’ll let you know by holding the palms of my hands out against my chest and that’ll be a signal to let you know it’s time to stop.”

Sometimes Neal would write down his feelings on paper to Cathie, so he wouldn’t get frustrated by her response. You may find other new ways of communicating and this should help to rebuild relationships and give others a new understanding of what you’re going through and a new perspective on how they should react to it.

Note: It’s easier for someone to care about you when they’ve been allowed to enter into your world through communication.

‘No one understands!’

I think that statement goes hand in hand with no one cares, but there's an additional questionable clause to it. How can they possibly understand when they're not you, or going through the horrors you've faced and are still facing?

The only way Neal could grasp what others were thinking when understanding or not understanding him was by trying to step outside his inner self and look back in. Neal said that he did this by imagining he was talking to a deaf person who couldn't use sign language and the only way they could communicate was to write things down.

These are the questions he wrote to himself: 'Would I be patient with how long it took for them to tell me a long story?'

'Would I feel inadequate when I couldn't quite grasp the meaning behind what they'd written?'

'Would they feel frustrated by me not being able to respond in the way they're expecting me to?'

You see, Neal figured this out: if he couldn't grasp their exact feelings and thoughts, it wasn't because he didn't care; it was just that he wasn't them. Once he began to step out of himself and see how he was acting, he could also grasp Cathie's frustration when trying to communicate with him. Cathie's frustration and sensitivity was never about how Neal was reacting, but about how she felt; she was failing and wishing the whole time she could do things better. Once he understood this, then he knew they both had to meet somewhere in the middle to move forward.

'I'll never regain my cognitive ability!'

Not true: Neal is writing books, speaking at presentations with Cathie on the subject of PTSD, and mentoring staff in better ways to help people with PTSD and is now counselling.

'I'll never be able to step outside the house!'

Not true: Neal has done that and says he now gets bored when he has to stay home.

'People are looking at me and it makes me anxious!'

It still bothers Neal, but only minutely. He claims that's normal for people to be curious, and they'll do that anyway.

'I'll never be able to cope with what I've seen and heard again!'

Not true! Neal still has some flashbacks, but he now sees them as any other bad memory that almost everyone has. He focuses on the here-and-now and believes the flashbacks are past events.

'These nightmares will never go away!'

Neal says many of the nightmares have gone and some still remain, but far less frequent than before. What's far more important in Neal's eyes is learning more about them and developing techniques to overcome them, like calming himself down and refocusing thoughts toward a happier place. As time has gone on, they've become far less terrifying and easier to handle. Neal points out, "If you work to be patient and slowly persistent with your disorder and focus on positive outcomes, things can slowly improve." When our thoughts push us too hard to achieve, we can trip over our own two feet.

HOW TO ANSWER A QUESTION OR AN UNREASONABLE STATEMENT WITH A CALM REASONABLE QUESTION

'Get over it or move on!'

I'm trying to; any suggestions that can help?

'You're overreacting!'

What makes you feel that?

'Aren't you over that yet?'

No, but I'm working on it; any ideas that would help?

'Why can't you just be normal?'

What's normal?

'Others have been through worse than you and they're ok!'

Who are these others? Maybe I can find out what techniques they used?

'Stop dwelling on the past!'

How much do you know about PTSD?

'It happened years ago!'

Can you please explain how that changes things for me in the here-and-now?

'I know how you feel!'

Can you please explain to me how I feel?

Normally, people who make these statements are often ignorant of what you're actually going through. The best way to work through this is: don't question yourself, but to question them in an unassuming way. The whole thing is that only you know what you're going through and what others negatively think is irrelevant.

PATIENCE

Having patience slowly brings rewards.

Plan small goals that will lead you to larger ones, which in turn will lead you to the final goal.

Reward yourself at the end of every goal.

Small goal = small reward.

Larger goal = larger reward.

Final goal = the largest reward of all, overcoming the worst of PTSD.

Like any disability, not everyone will fully recover, but that doesn't mean you'll never be able to function on some level.

When someone loses both their legs, they may not be able to run fast like they used to, but they can still function and do many of the other things they used to. That didn't happen overnight but with patience, determination and hard work they eventually got there.

Each goal can be broken down into categories of your choice. Make them what's comfortable for you and **when** it's comfortable for you.

Neal's individualised goals: first one of all was leaving the house.

Number two: seeing a doctor, then a psychiatrist and then a psychologist.

Number three: going to a coffee shop.

Number four: going to a larger shop where he'd need to walk around.

Number five: going to a shopping centre or mall.

Number six: while at the mall, look for triggers.

Number seven: use distractions and breathing techniques to overcome anxiety attacks.

Number eight: follow number seven's methods with nightmares.

Each one of these could be jumbled around to suit individual symptoms, but the initial focus should remain on the targeted one.

No one should ever think these will work overnight, but positive change did happen for Neal over time and he believes it can also happen for others.

FOCUS

The main focus should be on what you can do, not what you can't, so don't consider your goal as unattainable, provided the goal you set is a realistic one. If it seems too extreme to reach or comprehend, then it probably is, but often this is only temporary if we remain patient and focus on smaller goals initially.

At the beginning of Neal's journey, he didn't have a problem getting out of bed, but getting out of his pyjamas and into some clothes seemed impossible. All day long he'd either sit on the veranda or on the bed and just hypnotically stare at the scenery outside. So, when Cathie came home from shopping one day and saw him dressed, she almost cried. Little things mean a lot and when they remain consistent, they mean a lot more.

COMMUNICATION CAN BE SO HELPFUL IF USED CORRECTLY

Both Cathie and Neal agree on the above statement, especially when working as counsellors. Being good communicators was imperative when trying to gain ground on the perplexing issues they'd come across most working days.

How does this help with PTSD? Cathie makes the point that when Neal first went deep inside himself with PTSD, he didn't want to communicate at all, he just wanted to be his normal self again and because of the intense feelings he had inside, his patience was short. He knew if he communicated his frustration, he would make a mess of it, so instead of opening up, he'd shut down and walk away so he wouldn't offend his wife. Cathie on the other hand had trouble understanding what he was feeling during the initial part of their journey; I mean, how do we get to know people without being able to ask questions or them not being able to answer or both? From her perspective, Cathie understood it was about being patient and just making gentle, short statements like: “Dinner is ready.”, “Your show is on.”, “I’ll be out the back if you need me.” etc., then it was just a matter of waiting for Neal to ask her something.

This worked in two ways. The first way was it prevented overreaction from Neal and the second was it started him questioning why she was being straight to the point. This then led to a small form of distraction away from his confused mind, requiring him to question her motives for these out of character actions, leading him to ask the question, “Are you ok?” her response, “Yes, I’m fine.” This would then be followed by a curious smile and an open question, which would encourage Neal to give an answer, “That’s an odd question, what made you ask that?” Neal would initially give a short answer like, “It’s alright, it’s just me.” And instead of Cathie continuing to push the issue, she’d simply say,

"Ok." And leave it at that, which again would be out of character for Cathie.

As Cathie continued with her short and to the point answers, the more Neal's responses grew. Over time Neal would not only open up to the psychologist, but conversations grew in the Davies home.

So, what are open-ended and closed-ended questions?

Open-ended questions are questions that can't be answered with a simple yes or no answer and require the responder to elaborate their response.

These questions will often start with the words: How? What? When? Where? and Why?

Closed-ended questions mostly lead to yes or no answers.

These questions will often begin with the words: Did? Would? Do? and Are?

So using open-ended questions when speaking to someone with PTSD can help to motivate awareness, encourage thought and conversation, but it must be done with moderation and awareness of the person with PTSD's rationality and if done in the initial stages of the disorder, it's wise to keep statements short and to the point until they're ready to open up. What's even more important during the initial stages of the disorder is to ensure the person is taken to a doctor quickly to get a diagnosis.

WHAT WAS CONTAINED IN THE DIARY OR LOGBOOK YOU KEPT, NEAL?

I guess many of the things written here and in the first book were listed and used, but the really important ones to me were: making a list of the things I was avoiding and then focusing on them one at a time. Because of the state I was in, I would take each one apart piece by piece. For example: How did I feel about going to this place before PTSD? What's changed about that particular place to make me want to avoid it? Does this avoidance have anything to do with reality? What would help me in these circumstances?

Because I was battling with mixed emotions pulsating through my thoughts, I felt that by keeping things simple and exploring one issue at a time, it made it less likely to stir up frustration and anger and a little easier to focus. This system of breaking down the things I was avoiding, not only helped me mend many of the anxiety issues I had with leaving the house or going to shopping malls, but it also could be converted into searching out triggers and breaking down flash-backs.

Every day in my logbook I kept a record of how I was feeling, what I'd done for that day and how the day turned out. Then at the end of the month, I'd go back over the days and the weeks to look for movements, either positive or negative. That way I could summarise what was working and what wasn't and then make the appropriate adjustments. I'd also write down the consistency of nightmares I was having. Were they accumulating or easing? I would check on my consistency with daily rituals, and find new ones as I advanced.

I would write down the things that Cathie did that annoyed me and communicate them to her and how it affected me, and if I couldn't explain why it affected me, let her know that, and that I was still working on it to try and find out why. I'd write down the positives she was doing and thank her for them and let her know how I was always waiting for a time to talk to her, when I was feeling emotionally steady.

I'd write down songs that relaxed me and play them when I was tense until the stress went away and also play special songs that made me feel like I was in another place and time and I'd continue to play them frequently, until they became entrenched in my head.

As my confidence grew and my head became clearer, so would the challenges I'd place on myself, while also monitoring what I felt was the most important thing of all, my awareness. I knew as the awareness of my thoughts grew, so would my ability to self-analyse and understand if they were plausible thoughts, and if they weren't, I could examine them and focus on their meaning and their relation to what had happened to me during my trauma.

The logbook helped me so much over the years, and it's really important for the reader to understand that PTSD doesn't just pack its cases and leave the next morning; the time of its stay will vary from case to case, due to each individual and each individual's trauma, and some people can deal with trauma better than others. PTSD in some cases can last only months and others can last years, and this is one of the reasons I continue to emphasise to the reader that those with initial PTSD should immediately seek professional help.

One reminder written at regular intervals in the logbook was, '**We can't achieve everything we want**

to achieve overnight, but we can set small consistent tasks which will lead to our goals.'

Keeping the journal had so many benefits for me, especially in the early stages of my chronic PTSD. At that point I'd lost all confidence in myself and even after coming through the worst of it, I was having mental blanks during conversations with others that I wasn't close to.

What I did find though, was that whenever I was writing in the logbook I could think and write without hesitation or blocks to my thoughts. Writing also gave me a certain amount of relief from flashbacks and anxiety attacks, so I would then use it as another tool to overcome the worst of my condition. Even today I continue to keep a journal (diary) and use it like a mirror to reflect good and bad changes that may occur in my everyday patterns to help me keep good awareness and focus on how I'm handling life in general.

I guess I compare what I do regarding my disorder to how I treat my car; early patterns may show no signs of issues on a regular basis and then one day I may hear a rattling noise, so I get it fixed before it becomes a major concern. So to me, my journal does a similar job; it helps me pick up any minor issues so I can fix them rather than let them fester.

LIVING AND WORKING WITH A DISABILITY

It's ok to remind yourself that it's not impossible to live and work with a disability at the same time. People in wheelchairs do it, blind people do it and many people with different mental illnesses do it, but the one thing the majority of them have in common is that they know their limitations and their awareness is the key to that knowledge.

I believe it's important to ask yourself: "Are you aware of what you're capable of doing?" In other words, now that you feel on top of things, is there anything that still needs improvement for you to accomplish what you used to do, and if not, are there new ways of approaching it without taking away vital pieces which could detrimentally affect the end result or others?

Neal commented that in the very beginning of his chronic PTSD, all he wanted to do was to be able to think clearly so he could go straight back to counselling. Can you imagine that? He walks straight back into a session knowing exactly how to go about counselling and halfway through the session, he has a flash-back which creates an anxiety attack. In this type of scenario, it would seem like he was back to normality when he entered the session, but in reality, his awareness of limitations and overall aspects of his position was lacking. So, as much as he desperately wanted to do something that he did before his disorder, before he could do it, he needed to look at every aspect of both what was required from him in his past position, and also what he was capable of doing at that very time. Neal said this was done by asking himself, "What symptoms of my disorder will interfere with what's required of me in my past position?" Obviously, Neal understood how going back too soon could not only do detrimental damage to his own movement forward from his disorder, but also, the negative and detrimental effect it could have on his clients as well.

At the beginning, when Neal wanted to go back to work, he was so confused that he withdrew into himself and couldn't even consider doing it; in fact he didn't even want to leave the house, but once Cathie got him to see a professional, his awareness slowly began to return and he was grateful that Cathie hadn't debated his desire to go back. As a counsellor herself, she just calmly asked the right questions about how he would cope if…? and once he couldn't answer those imperative questions about his position, he began to realise he couldn't go back to work until he could clearly focus on those certain individual issues that were still blocking his progress forward. Neal realised that if he was going to get back to the career he loved, he'd have to overcome each and every one of his symptoms to a point where he could cope with them in the worst case scenarios; something he eventually did after thirteen years and was then cleared to go back to work.

Into the later stages of his journey, an incident happened close to Neal and Cathie that would unnerve the best of us. I think by telling you this story, you may get some comprehension of the determination and resolve Neal possesses to get through an incident that would shake up most people without PTSD, let alone someone with it.

Neal and Cathie were sitting at a table having a cappuccino in the centre walkway of a mall, when a young lady and her little boy walked past Neal and Cathie's table. Just as they passed, a large square piece of the roof fell down, crashing to the floor beside them, with a huge bang. Cathie almost jumped from her seat initially, but then looked instinctively to Neal and saw he was as white as a ghost and she asked him if he was ok and if he'd like to leave. She could see he'd gone quite pale and his hands were shaking a little, but not to the extreme and he replied, "No, I don't want to go, I need to see this through." Neal then went silent for approximately five minutes, until the colour finally came back into his face. From the moment it happened, to the moment that Neal's colour had returned to his face, Neal said he'd focused on his breathing by taking deep breaths through his nose and breathing out through his mouth. He also thought positive thoughts such as 'It's passed, and everyone's alright.' and then made a joke of what had just happened in his head, 'Wow, what a way to ruin an enjoyable coffee!' After the event they both talked about the incident and how close it came to the young lady and her child. Cathie later said she was more prepared to 'get out of there' after the incident than Neal was.

Neal has continued to say, "If I had followed my instincts and gone back to work when I hadn't covered all of my issues, I feel it may have set me back further and I believe my self-confidence would have dropped to an all-time low. Don't get me wrong, there were setbacks along the way but that was a matter of readjustment, and readjustments are imperative when it comes to rehabilitation, but to try and do it during a counselling career, you don't have that sort of leeway to play with."

Some may see Neal's views and goals as 'over the top', but he saw them as a way of having as close to full rehabilitation as he felt he could possibly get. He still accepts there's left-over residue of his disorder, but he now feels he's at a point where his 'awareness' of all his PTSD symptoms and the work he's done, on each and every one of them, has given him control over what once were immediate reactions or reflex-instincts. He also felt that using positive reinforcement with the line, "This is today and what happened then isn't happening now!" helped ease the constant overwhelming negatives from reappearing time and time again. He found putting this collection (although challenging) of refocusing tools into his armoury became a major player in finding his 'new normality.' He knew nothing would ever be the same, but whatever is? His focus wasn't on what was, but what could be.

Neal continues to say, "We grow older, don't we, and don't we have to adapt with age? Every day brings new challenges throughout our lives, some we've faced before and have solutions for, and they eventually become comfortable to deal with. Then, there are new ones that aren't so comfortable, until they are."

HERE'S A CRAZY EXAGGERATED HYPOTHETICAL FOR YOU

Imagine a skydiver crashing into a tree at the end of his free-fall and because of the impact he has some fairly serious head injuries which cause him some memory loss and a broken leg after cutting himself free of the tree and falling to the ground.

After coming out of hospital he's also diagnosed with PTSD and acrophobia (the fear of heights). Once he's healed from his physical injuries, he sets about getting over his PTSD and acrophobia as quickly as possible, because he has such a passion for skydiving and he wants to get that amazing sensation back. The first step he literally takes is on the first rung of a ladder and he stands there until his hands and feet stop shaking. Over a period of a month, the task gets harder and harder as he climbs higher and higher on the ladder. Eventually, after sometimes not being able to cope and coming down during his bouts of anxiety, he finally makes it to the top of the ladder and throws his hands into the air in celebration.

His next goal takes him to the top of a skyscraper, and he spends each day working his way closer and closer to the edge. Once he conquers that, he feels that he is ready, but to make sure he's definitely ready to make that jump, he decides to take three joy flights to get the feel of the distance from the plane to the ground. After the third flight, he's ready and raring to go and once that door is opened and he's called forward, he has no inhibitions about what he's about to do at all. He flies out of the plane like a swallow with a huge, flapping smile stretched right across his face. Several other student skydivers follow with their instructor. As he falls, he's amazed at what he's accomplished to be there, and as he looks around in awe at the amazing scenery below, he suddenly catches sight of the instructor leveling with him and pointing to his own ripcord. Realising he hasn't pulled it, he has a flash-back from his initial trauma and once anxiety kicks in he begins to panic; the instructor immediately flies in and grabs hold of him in a hugging position and pulls the cord for him and then let's go and pulls his own as well. Luckily both chutes open in the nick of time and both men land safely.

Although this is truly an over-exaggerated hypothetical, there are still lessons to be learned in it; once your awareness kicks in, don't push to get back into your old normality too quickly. Once you've overcome one part of the disorder, look for any others that may hold you back when you think you're ready to move forward.

Don't be distracted from your goal by wanting to achieve it too quickly and don't be afraid or embarrassed to get a professional's opinion on where they think you're at with your condition. Sometimes it's easier to have others look from the outside in, than to look for yourself from the inside out. Simply put, sometimes it's easier for someone else to pick up on something we've overlooked, when we're being too eager to get back to something we've lost.

The whole point is: what's happening to us is very new and we need time to adjust to what we're feeling emotionally. If we don't give ourselves that initial time to adjust, it'll take longer to overcome than it normally should. We need to stop pushing to get back to normality and allow ourselves the time it takes to recover fully, or else we may overload our mind and miss the important things that we need for our journey forward.

Eventually, the skydiver takes a break from skydiving for a while until he's regained full memory function and also worked to overcome the majority of what was triggering the flashbacks and anxieties.

How important is communication when it comes to PTSD?

The not-so-funny thing about PTSD is that it can hold you back from communicating when you most need to. Neal said he'd lost count of the number of people who don't have the disorder, yet want to know how it affects people and why many of them seem angry or withdrawn. His explanation to them was this: imagine hitting your hand with a hammer or accidentally scalding yourself with boiling water, and then someone comes up to you out of concern, and keeps asking over and over again: "Are you ok?” Although it’s not a physical pain you’re going through, it’s a very similar emotional pain - only more. As much as you understand they're doing this because they care, what they don't understand is that at this very decisive moment your emotions are screaming over the top of any logic you have left, and you just want them to go away until the emotional pain subsides.

The people Neal speaks to now with PTSD, say they feel exactly the same way: extreme out of control inner emotion without that extreme pain, and it can be ongoing for much of the day, every day, so naturally the last thing on their minds is wanting to communicate with anyone. It's not that they're angry with you and it's not that they want to deliberately dismiss you by responding negatively or just walking away; it's just that they have very little control over their inner frustrations. Although it isn’t easy, all anyone can do is try not to take it personally, step back and observe, and then communicate when the time is right. So in reality, there will be times where those with the disorder may not have full control over their own behaviour.

Having chronic PTSD as a counsellor, Neal now feels fortunate in a way, because he had the knowledge of what to do with certain aspects of this crippling disorder, but even that wasn't enough. Neal continued to work diligently to develop many of his own techniques, which he now shares with professionals. What he also sees as a positive aspect of his journey, is having his counsellor wife by his side and who remained there throughout the entire thirteen-year journey. Cathie had given up her career to become his carer and helped him through it all. Cathie also learned how hard it could be to be a carer, so she also worked to develop new techniques from a carer's perspective on when and how to initially converse with someone going through the first stages of the disorder.

Both Cathie and Neal now do talks to both carers and those with PTSD. They also consult with other organisations to help enhance their awareness and skills when it comes to working with people with the disorder. We all have bumps in the road on our journeys through life. Some bumps are harsher than others, but if we don't look for the lessons buried in those potholes, we've missed some amazing ideas and techniques, and our journeys become worthless and nothing more than a bad memory of a bumpy road.

Cathie is now back into counselling and working with Neal. They constantly come together to do presentations for people with PTSD, and carers too. They give those who attend a better understanding of what both the carer and those with the disorder are going through on their own journey of healing.

Cathie, through her business (Beyond PTSD), is also helping counsellors and carers alike on how to approach and have a better understanding of those with PTSD through her knowledge and lived experience.

Neal is also back counselling, something that seemed like a pipe dream to him and many others at the beginning of his journey. Neal's lived experience with his own chronic PTSD and his knowledge of counselling helps those that he sees during counselling sessions to have a better understanding of dealing with their own PTSD.

REFLECTING

When Cathie was asked what she did to help with communication in the middle stages of Neal's disorder, she responded with reflecting or paraphrasing. This technique is often used in counselling and it's used by repeating back the meaning of the sentence used by the other person, only with different words. This technique should be used sparingly, or it will become an annoyance rather than a help to both you and them.

So, how does it work? And how does it help?

What Cathie would do was this: when Neal made a statement such as, "I'm still having a bit of trouble thinking clearly now, but it has got better!"

Cathie may respond with, “So, even though you’re still having problems with your thinking, it has improved, right?”

This way Cathie wasn’t only clarifying Neal’s statement, but she was also showing him she was listening and also understanding what had been said to her. Cathie said she’d then add a positive spin with a statement followed by an open-ended question like this one: “I’ve seen you go through so much and come so far, so how does it feel to be able to look back and know how far you’ve come?”

Cathie went on to say, “The way we communicate with someone with PTSD can positively or negatively shape the conversation and define whether or not the conversation will continue or shut down immediately.”

Let’s have a look at some of the **NEGATIVES** Cathie tried to avoid:

- Aggressive or loud tones
- Jumping in before Neal had finished his sentence

- Angry expressions
- Disinterested expressions
- Being easily distracted while Neal was speaking
- Overtalking or constant repetition

Cathie went on to explain: there'll always be slip-ups, but as a carer we can only do what we can. What we need to understand is that somebody with PTSD is super-sensitive, and often conversations can be short and sweet. As they improve and regain much of the confidence they'd lost, the conversations from them can become rapid and long as though they haven't spoken in years.

Let's now have a look at some of the **POSITIVES** Cathie tried to implement:

- Listen with interest

Listening gives the other person the opportunity to express their feelings.

Listening effectively gives us the opportunity to learn more about them and their feelings.

- Listen with empathy

Although we can never understand what a person has been through or is going through, we can listen to what they want to communicate to us and help them to see they're not alone on the journey. Just a simple, "Wow! You've had a lot on your plate, haven't you?" gives those going through trauma a supportive and non-judgmental response to their words.

- Give positive feedback without being patronising

Too many sympathetic words in our response can seem patronising to someone who's been through a lot, at times it can even shut down communication and make them feel that you're not really interested. We can definitely show empathy, but in short bursts. This helps them open up to you more, allowing them to further their communication and rebuild confidence in themselves. Many people that go through trauma feel judged in everything they do and say, to open up to a non-judgmental person, who is listening to their deepest feelings, rebuilds their confidence and helps their healing process.

Don't take the emphasis off what they're going through by comparing negatively. Negative comparisons can make what happened to the trauma victim feel less and create a sense of distrust in those who use those negative comparisons. It can also make them withdraw from constructive communication.

Imagine a person who has been through a horrific, traumatic experience and gets diagnosed with PTSD, their anxiety is through the roof, certain sounds and places trigger flash-backs of the day it happened, and their nightmares are so real they don't know if they're awake or asleep. A couple of weeks pass; nothing seems to have improved, and their partner says to them, "Don't you think it's time to go back to work? I've had friends who've had PTSD and it hasn't taken them this long to get over it!" What we have to understand is, different things affect different people in different ways.

HYPOTHETICAL

Harry may love driving fast cars and has accidents on the racing tracks a bit; then one day Harry has a crash on a highway on the way home, he has a broken leg and facial injuries but feels fine mentally and has no signs of PTSD.

Harry may have also lost his young boy in a swimming pool incident and one day he's down by the river fishing and he notices a family further up from him having a picnic, all of a sudden something catches his eye and he spots a small boy around the same age as the son he'd lost. The boy's very close to the water's edge, so Harry screams out to the family and they race down to grab him just as he is about to fall in. Harry's past flashes before him, and he uncontrollably abuses them verbally and then packs up his gear and weeps all the way home in the car.

Yes, Harry did get over the car crash quickly as he was back racing cars when his wounds healed and he'd been through it all before but then something he never believed would happen actually happens, something that he has no understanding or control over and it shatters his entire world.

The lesson here is we should never make negative comparisons about trauma and rarely make a comparison with others who have suffered one unless helping someone to understand they're not alone on their journey and sharing ideas and techniques that may help with their trauma as well.

TIPS

The only time Neal says he makes a comparison, is when a person with PTSD asks him about what he'd been through with the aftermath of the incidents he attended and all he says is, triggers, anxiety, flash-backs and nightmares and when they say, “So you do understand!” he responds with: “I don’t understand exactly what you’re feeling or have been through, but I do understand how frightened and extreme it felt to me! What’s important for you to know is, you’re not alone!”

You need to know when to back off, especially if the person you are speaking to with PTSD seems annoyed or overwhelmed and allow them to open up if they feel the need.

Try to learn a bit about body language - it can really help when talking to someone who's been through trauma. Watch their face while you’re talking. Things like rapid breathing, a furrowed brow, or raised eyebrows can be signs of anxiety. Also, listen to how they speak. Their voice might sound shaky, louder than usual, or they might go quiet altogether. Nonverbal cues like these often say more than words.

Once you see a negative mood swing, it might help to ask a simple question such as: “Would you like to leave this conversation for now and come back to it later?" This way you're not just walking away, which could be misconstrued as fed up or angry with them; instead you're giving '**them**' the option to continue on or pull out of the conversation. Just walking away can diminish their control and make it too hard for them to come back to the discussion at a later time.

Never ever say "you should..." Suggestions are gentler than directives when faced with hyper-sensitive emotions and if 'most' people can, those with PTSD would if they only could. So for you to say, "You should!" to a person with PTSD can not only create anxiety but also frustration as well, especially when they try, and they can't.

TOGETHER

The PTSD journey is all but over for Neal and Cathie and they know something that most others would never consider when meeting and talking with Neal, and that is he still carries scars that are unlikely to ever heal but he's amazingly made them manageable.

Neal's graphic nightmares come and go, but nowhere near as often as they used to, and he deals with them much better than he did at the beginning of this long and remarkable journey. When they do occur, his immediate, trained thought reminds him they're not real and to slow his breathing and relax his body from the toes up; he also curls up in bed and thinks about rainy days, which has always relaxed him and then he goes back to sleep. The moment the nightmares happen, Cathie will give him a gentle pat on the back to comfort him until reality kicks back in.

Flashbacks are now like bad memories of the past that most people have, and Neal can talk about them but it's no more than a little uncomfortable to do so, like it is for anyone without PTSD. He also makes certain that the conversation regarding these past traumatic events, only goes on as long as he feels comfortable and/or no further than he wants it to. If it becomes too uncomfortable, he'll smile and let you know, and then he'll change the subject.

Over thirteen long years Neal had worked diligently to track down most of the triggers that were creating the flashbacks and even when faced with new ones, he no longer gets affected the way he used to. He always reminds himself he's in the here-and-now and what happened back then no longer exists. This isn't denial or blocking out of past traumas or they'd still be affecting him to the point where he wouldn't be coping at all in the here-and-now. Once he'd come through the initial 'Haze' with Cathie's help, he saw this as a challenge that he had to adopt new ways of approach using both old and new techniques combined.

Neal's anxiety now is very much back to his old normality. We all have some type of anxiety, but this is now controllable to the point where Cathie and Neal do talks in front of large groups of people on the subject of working through PTSD and caring for someone with PTSD. These talks have now helped so many people, which in turn continues to help them, as they now feel it's made their own arduous journey, with its important lessons, exceptionally worthwhile.

Neal's got on top of his PTSD with the help of his amazing wife Cathie and her initial push to get him out of the house and doing something different from what he was used to doing. This distracted him from focusing on getting back to something that he could no longer do at that point. It also helped to bring about new awareness and self-confidence and that awareness helped him to know his boundaries and capabilities, which brought about focus on small achievable goals and then onto larger ones.

When Cathie could see that much of Neal's past normality had returned, she went back into counselling part-time and then opened a business called Beyond PTSD based on Neal's first book

PTSD Not Just For Some But For Everyone and they haven't looked back.

Every single day is a Godsend to them and each time they see a glimmer of hope for those they're working with or talking to, it reminds them just why they needed to go through their own ordeal and their passion to help others continues to grow.

HOMEWARD BOUND

Leading up to the end of this long and arduous journey, Neal had chosen to make the last year of it slow and steady, while continuing to remain positive and excited. His confidence regarding his awareness had built up to the point where he deliberately began challenging himself to do difficult emotional tasks that he never would have considered at any other time during his journey with PTSD. Neal felt that this was essential if he wanted to return to the career he was so passionate about.

Throughout his career Neal always put his clients first and knew that if he wasn't capable of overcoming these difficult emotional tasks that he'd set himself, then he couldn't possibly overcome future obstacles which may appear in his work as a counsellor.

Since regularly challenging himself over a period of one year by starting with small challenges and gradually enlarging them as he went, Neal has found that he has very few of his original symptoms of chronic PTSD left. Nightmares have remained but only on very rare occasions and he has a method of overcoming their impact through breathing exercises that have become better through persistence and practice over the past thirteen years. Neal still has minor anxiety which only comes prior to speaking to an audience, but he always had this prior to PTSD and the anxiety fades away once he begins talking about his and Cathie's journey.

Neal's triggers and flashbacks have gone, but clear memories still remain of the traumatic events he faced all those years ago. The only difference now compared with then is, he can speak calmly about them, whereas before he'd break down or he wouldn't be able to finish explaining those traumatic events.

Neal acknowledges that, like anyone who has faced a traumatic or frightening event, some memories can be stressful. But their impact can also fade to a manageable level when you make up your mind to move those traumas out of the spotlight and take back control of your mind. This means taking the importance away from PTSD and putting it back on you, along with who you were before this rude intruder decided to interrupt your life journey.

After Neal had worked through all the things that may go wrong in a session, and he was absolutely sure that no harm would come to his clients, he began counselling once more and any doubts he'd had regarding his ability to resume his career completely disappeared.

Not only that, but the marathon journey had presented Neal with newfound techniques and skills that enhanced his previous ones way beyond his own beliefs and expectations. The more people he worked with, with PTSD, the more his confidence grew, and the people who came to see him found they had an immediate connection to him. Cathie says she's lost count of the people he's spoken to at meet and greets who say he truly understands so much of what they're going through and how they now believe there's light at the end of the tunnel for them.

Neal continues to give enormous credit to Cathie and believes he may have still been stuck in the early stages of his disorder without her love, devotion, skills and incredible patience. When asked about her stamina over the years and how she continued to cope, she made this comment: "It was hard at first and I desperately wanted my 'old

Neal' back, but in all honesty I knew at some point, he'd make it, because I knew him and when it comes to a challenge, he won't just throw in the towel. Neal has to know there's nothing left he can do to overcome his hurdles for him to even consider giving in, that's just who he is. I think for me though, when you love someone like I love Neal, what other option do you have but to help them all you can and continue to let them know you're there for them no matter what? At no point did I ever want to walk away from my wonderful husband and God gave me the strength to see it through."

Cathie had worked hard, patiently and persistently without forcing Neal to communicate. When he finally started to communicate again, she let him lead the way, and when she could see that he was becoming uncomfortable with it, she'd immediately back off and go about what she was doing before the conversation began.

CONCLUSION

During Neal and Cathie's journey, there were some huge setbacks. One of Neal's publishers went into liquidation temporarily, putting a halt to his writing of novels and prompting him to ask himself 'What next? What more can be taken from me?' Cathie stepped up to the plate and learned how to publish books, so it wouldn't happen again.

Before Cathie's mother died, there'd been some family issues and Neal stood by her side throughout, pushing many of his own issues aside to be there for hers.

Neither of them gave up on each other throughout their entire journey and yes, there were times when things got tough, but once they'd pushed through the obstacles together, it not only made them both individually stronger, but it also brought them closer together.

Note: Life would be boring if every single thing went to plan all the time, so when things go wrong, they make things feel so much better when they're over. It's our choice to push on or create our own victim.

It's been another seven long years since Neal wrote *PTSD Not Just For Some But For Everyone*, and both Cathie and Neal's lives have changed for the better in so many ways.

Prior to Covid, Neal had taken a bold step with Cathie's encouragement to form a joint effort, and they began doing presentations regarding their journey with PTSD, both from a person with the disorder and the carer of the person with the disorder and how they'd been moving forward by positively using old and new techniques to help them along the way. They only began giving these presentations after Neal had worked through many of his PTSD triggers and anxieties - the same ones that had stopped him from taking the first step toward sharing his story publicly.

Now it was time to take a minimal risk. With Cathie's encouragement and Neal's trust in God, he swallowed his fears and took the first step toward freedom of a disorder that kept him locked within himself for many, many years. While locked away, he'd never stopped examining and focusing on ways to escape his disorder, and Cathie had never given up on helping him gently push through barriers he'd never imagined could be conquered. Neal once said, "I may never leave some parts of PTSD behind, but I'll make sure the parts that remain will be manageable and under my control."

Once they had worked through their speeches and agreed they had got it right, they began presenting them at three venues and spoke to people who had either been a family carer, friend, or loved one of someone who had PTSD and also those who were suffering from the disorder itself. During and after their presentations, they realised just how successful and how needed these connective forums were. They were inundated with personal stories and questions of how they'd worked through particular aspects of Neal's PTSD and also how Cathie had managed to cope as Neal's carer. After three successful forums, Covid hit, bringing their work to an abrupt halt and leaving both of them wondering: what next? It didn't seem as big of a deal to Neal as it was to Cathie, as he pointed out he'd been used to inhabiting his inner self, although he was still enjoying the long drives and listening to interesting conversations.

Once Covid had passed, Cathie found Neal had taken a step backward and was again reluctant to mingle among large crowds that you find in shopping centres and crowded streets. Neal said his withdrawal from public life was self-imposed as he was really struggling with his emotions and some depression. He went on to say that the thought of being locked away during Covid brought him undone, as he and Cathie had both worked so hard to get him out of the house and back into public life. Neal had already pushed himself through a very tough period of his life and the break with lockdowns saw him withdraw from what he and

Cathie had accomplished regarding presentations on PTSD.

Once the lockdowns were finally lifted, Cathie came to the fore by choosing the right times to encourage him to join her in what he saw as daunting places, and backing off when she could see he just wasn't coping. At this point they'd both seemed to have given up on the idea of revisiting the forums, even though they knew they'd helped so many of those who'd attended the events, but it seemed God had other ideas of where and what they should be doing. Everything unfolded when a good friend who was familiar with Neal's first book and their journey, asked them to attend a meeting where a large group of people were gathering and speaking on the prevention of suicide.

While they were there, mingling and talking to others, an ABC radio presenter from Cairns, who was travelling around the outback towns of North Queensland and getting stories, just happened to be interviewing people in their tiny town of Mount

Morgan and had been encouraged to go to where the meeting was taking place. That's when he overheard Neal and Cathie speaking to some others who were present; he was so intrigued by their story he asked them if they'd be interested in giving him an interview. How could they not then see that their journey from before Covid needed to be continued? So, from there they were off and running again and as they put it, "We'll continue to do so, knowing it's our calling, and the bonus is the benefit it's bringing to others!"

After that experience with the lockdowns, Neal now points out to others with PTSD, "Don't feel bad if things aren't moving as fast as you'd like; there'll always be holdups and hurdles along the way and once they're out of the way, off you go again!"

Cathie agrees and has a similar philosophy, she says, "Even from a carer's position, I couldn't make things go any faster. Pushing Neal forward when he wasn't ready would only do the opposite. You can't make others change pace, it's up to them how fast or slow they go, but you can encourage them."

Whether you have PTSD or not, there are some things in this life that will set you back and you can either accept their control over you or you can take that control back; it all comes down to your choice. Most problems can be solved or resolved over time and being patient is the key. Once we take a different view on how to solve these problems, we tend to study how others have got through or overcome them. The issue or problem may never be resolved completely, but with what has been achieved in their research and efforts, it can become functional; a legless man can still walk, can't he?

I think the thing that frustrates both Neal and Cathie most is the lack of attention and detail given to carers. When people read about or hear a story about someone who has PTSD, the immediate focus mostly centres either on what had happened to that person and how it has affected 'them' but rarely describes the impact it's had on the entire family. There are some exceptions to this, like major court cases or noted people, whose family are interviewed in the media and get the chance to explain the impact that it's also had on them, but there are so many wonderful people working diligently to help their loved ones through trauma, while they suffer in silence.

Both Neal and Cathie emphasise that those working through this journey with clients need to remain aware of the fact that PTSD not only affects those who've been through a trauma, but also those who are affected by their loved one's trauma; husbands, wives, children, and any other relative or friend who has a close bond with them. If at this time 11% of all Australians have PTSD, imagine the number of loved ones, who are affected indirectly through seeing and feeling the emotional pain they're witnessing. How many suffer in silence through it all, while having the dilemma of trying to be strong for those they are so close to? All the while being torn up inside with their own emotional pain, when seeing the persona of someone they love totally change - never knowing if the person they once knew will ever return. This is why Cathie created her business based on Neal's book and called it "Beyond PTSD". Neal and Cathie both believed that if they were going to make more effective inroads into this debilitating disorder, they should not only focus on those with PTSD, but also focus on helping those who don't understand or know how to cope with the drastic change in someone they love. It wouldn't be difficult at all to continue on with what they've accomplished with their presentations and meet and greets, with other organisations since. What they see as more important is teaching people how they've arrived at where they are now, and the techniques they used. They also answer these types of questions that are asked at their presentations.

Neal is now back counselling and helping others in the sector. He has also reactivated his membership with the Australian Counsellors Association.

Neal and Cathie reflect on the thirteen years that they dedicated to each other and this arduous journey. They also reflect on how it feels to be coping and cleared to be doing what they both love best; helping others.

Neal makes it very clear that he couldn't have come this far without the love and dedication that his wife gave throughout. He said Cathie's patience and persistence to help him push through extraordinary barriers was astonishing and she was his rock throughout it! Cathie said it was hard for both of them and if people had only seen how bad Neal was at the start of it all, they would never have believed he'd come out of it.

Even though he'd put on a façade to family and friends, he never expressed how extreme the horrific nightmares were or the anxiety attacks that made him pale, shake and walk away from her so she couldn't see him cry. There were triggers that created his anxiety and flashbacks that he fought off most days of the week. Even Cathie said that to see it first-hand was heartbreaking, and most people wouldn't have realised what he was actually going through and covering up, just so he didn't feel foolish or offend others. Cathie went on to say that she couldn't believe how emotionally weak and yet instinctively strong he was to get through it all; and when asked, he also gave some of the credit to his father.

Neal had told Cathie that his father was a drover's son and had seen some pretty tough times himself, and when Neal was a child and fell down skinning his knee, his father would tell him to "Get up, it doesn't hurt that much!" And although he didn't appreciate it at the time, those words would pop into his mind whenever something too difficult would crop up and much of the time, he'd find a way through it.

Cathie stated she was so proud of her husband and what he's achieved, and given the degree of his chronic PTSD, it says so much to so many others trying to ride out the storm and for those who care for them.

Neal also gives enormous credit to his wife and the patience, love and persistence to not only stick it out but to also implant positive techniques that helped him get through the very worst of the initial phase he was going through.

The aim of Neal and Cathie is to continue to help others going through this ordeal, both carers and sufferers alike; they want them to understand that they're not alone and to not give up on each other but join forces to beat it together.

FROM US TO YOU

Throughout your journey, your mind will challenge you as it did with us, but always remember, you're not alone. If we survived, both as someone with this emotionally crippling disorder and as a carer whose life changed overnight, so can you.

We care about those reading this book, because at some point in a lifetime, we're all affected by big or small traumas. To some, these traumas are just bad memories; to others they can linger. If we can help shorten that period of lingering time with the techniques we've written here, then we feel we've done what we set out to do and we'll also know that you will no longer feel alone.

Made in United States
North Haven, CT
04 November 2026

21772744R00124